Dragon Man: An Actor's Transformation

Everyone Be***lie***ves Their Own Story

Dragon Man: An Actor's Transformation

Everyone Be*lie*ves Their Own Story

Jai Tatsuto West

Essentia

London, UK

Washington, DC, USA

CollectiveInk

First published by Essentia Books, 2026
Essentia Books is an imprint of Collective Ink Ltd.,
Unit 11, Shepperton House, 89 Shepperton Road, London, N1 3DF
office@collectiveinkbooks.com
www.collectiveinkbooks.com
www.essentia-books.com

For distributor details and how to order, please visit the 'Ordering' section on our website.

ISBN: 978 1 917704 13 7
978 1 917704 18 2 (ebook)
Library of Congress Control Number: 2025933047

A CIP catalogue record for this book is available from the British Library.

Design: Lapiz Digital Services

Author photo by Kohki Hasei

UK: Printed and bound by CPI Group (UK) Ltd, Croydon, CR0 4YY
Printed in North America by CPI GPS partners

The manufacturer's authorised representative in the EU for product safety is:
eucomply OÜ - Pärnu mnt 139b-14, 11317 Tallinn, Estonia, hello@ eucompliancepartner.com,
www.eucompliancepartner.com

Previous Works

Jai West has released two albums of poetry under the pseudonym LOTUS CHAMELiON:

i once loved an egyptian queen (2002)
Transcend Records (JP) / TRAG-2201

SOLILOQUi (2004)
Transcend Records (JP) / TRAG-4201

In 2024, he released the single *Dragon of Possibility: Act 1 Spoken Things,*
a prelude to this book.

Ave Maria

Well, I am the one who loves changing from nothing to one.
Leonard Cohen

Contents

Prologue

In Japanese, the word for "seahorse" is *tatsu-no-otoshigo*, which literally translates to "fallen child of the dragon," reflecting the seahorse's unique appearance reminiscent of a dragon. In Japan, seahorses are children of dragons born above the clouds and dropped into the sea.

The seahorse is known for its distinctive habit of swimming upright with its head held high, often ascending toward the water's surface. Cherished in Japanese culture, it is a symbol of good luck, as its appearance evokes the image of a "rising dragon."

1

Pattern of Story

Susanoo, the storm god, wreaked havoc on the world, summoning violent storms that claimed lives and instilled terror in all. His tempestuous behavior frightened his sister, Amaterasu, the sun goddess, compelling her to retreat into a cave and shrouding the world in darkness. In the absence of her light, chaos reigned supreme. Alone in the heavens, Susanoo found himself at a crossroads, realizing that his triumph felt hollow without Amaterasu by his side.

After much persuasion from the other gods, Amaterasu emerged from her cave, bringing sunlight back to the world. Susanoo harbored hopes of her forgiveness, but instead, she returned with a formidable army of 800 gods, furious and ready for retribution. They descended upon him, inflicting brutal punishment as they tore at his beard and fingernails. His cries of anguish echoed in the cosmos as they bound him and presented the wounded Susanoo before Amaterasu.

"Send me down to Yomi, the land of the dead. I wish to be with our mother," he begged.

"Yomi is too good for you," Amaterasu replied sternly. "You have wrought unimaginable destruction upon mortals. Until you learn to respect and cherish their lives, you shall dwell among them, stripped of your divine powers and abilities. No storms, no godly might."

"Please, no! I am truly sorry!" Susanoo pleaded, but Amaterasu had grown weary of his empty vows of remorse.

With a mighty throw, the assembled kami (gods) cast Susanoo down to Earth. Wounded and humbled, he awoke on the coast of Izumo, stripped of his powers and embarrassed to find himself a god exiled from heaven. The gentle waves lapped at the shore, a reminder of the command he had lost, leaving him disoriented and adrift. In his solitude, he pondered, "What is it that the mortals need from me?

Amaterasu! What can I do to make things right? I will do anything — I will apologize to every single mortal I have wronged."

In the distant ocean the sunlight glittered on the water and it caught Susanoo's eye. Was the glittering sunbeam a coincidence? Or was Amaterasu giving him a sign?

Tails of Two Dragons

My name is Jai Tatsuto West, and I'm a half Japanese, half French-Canadian actor and poet. My mother, Masako Iijima, was born in Kuki-shi, Saitama-ken, in 1945, the Year of the Chicken. By the time she was 19, both of her parents had passed away, and she took on the responsibility of raising her two younger brothers. She worked as a telephone operator and narrator for overseas reports at Kyodo News in Ginza, where she met a Canadian man, Malcolm Wright, at the International Bureau. His one-year contract ended with a transfer to Washington, DC, and my mother, following her intuition, decided to cross the ocean and move to North America with him. Unfortunately, that relationship didn't last — Malcolm Wright turned out to be Malcolm Wrong.

A year later, now in Vancouver, BC, my mother made the bold decision not to return to Japan, and instead, she chose to stay in Canada and build a new life. It was there that she met and charmed my father, Claude Cecil West, a charismatic Bible salesman with the gift of gab, who was born in the Year of the Snake. A different book for another time.

When I share my mother's story with Japanese people, they are often amazed by her courage, she was one of the few who left Japan to seek a new beginning. She's a five-foot-tall Japanese woman with an accent — vibrant and fearless — who faced and embraced the unknown, and in doing so, created me. In the Chinese zodiac, there exists but one imaginary creature, I was born in the Year of the Dragon, and my mother gave me the middle name Tatsuto, which combines the Japanese words for "Dragon" and "Man." It's said that Dragon men can be intense — either incredibly good or terribly bad.

As far back as I can remember, my mother would often ask me, "*Jai-kun,* are you a rising dragon or a falling dragon?" With a gentle smile, she would add, "A rising dragon flies all the way to Heaven." But then, her tone would shift, and she'd warn, "If you're not careful, you'll become a falling dragon, and a falling dragon just keeps falling – DOWN, DOWN into the abyss, into the depths of Hell!" It frightened me. As a child, kind mom and strict mom seemed like two different people. It takes young children time to understand that both sides are part of the same whole. Even now, she continues to ask me this question, and its significance hasn't faded. It makes me reflect on my own path: am I headed North or South? Inside all of us, there are two dragons, both vying for direction.

I was born and raised in Vancouver, BC, Canada, and my childhood was truly idyllic. I attended a French Immersion Catholic elementary school called École St. Sacrement, which had its own French parish church. I served as an altar boy, sometimes helping with morning mass before classes started. I was captivated by the rituals – the behind-the-scenes preparations, the priest donning his purple robe, the lighting of the candles, the scent of burning incense, and the sound of the congregation as they filled the church. I would ring the bell to signal the start of the worship, and the altar felt like a stage where I could enact these sacred rituals. I assisted with communion, standing next to the priest and holding a gold plate beneath each person's mouth to catch any crumbs as Father Goddard served the Eucharist.

While mass was not my first experience with performance, it certainly gave me the familiar sensation that something meaningful was happening. I loved the attention; I felt as if I were embodying something important. In many ways, the priests were like actors in a symbolic play. The mass served to awaken our innate connection to the transcendent, creating a powerful experience for those attending.

The best part about being an altar boy was, after mass, one might receive a little cash – usually two or five dollars. If I was lucky, a wedding would net me ten or even twenty dollars. It was pocket money I could take to the corner store for candy.

Sometimes, I would linger alone in the church, making the rounds and gazing at the beautiful, brutal depictions of the fourteen stations of the cross. These images told the story of the Passion of Christ, revealing the suffering of the crucifixion. In those moments, I felt so bad for Jesus, I couldn't fathom the evil that he confronted. Above the altar in our Blessed Sacrament Parish church, the main crucifix portrayed the resurrected Jesus, arms wide open, radiant and smiling. I could feel the sacred presence as I gazed at the crucifix and even at that young age, I knew what it meant, that even in the darkest times, there is always hope.

My mother volunteered as the assistant librarian at the school library, or "bibliothèque" in French. My first class every day was Catechism, where we studied the Bible. Basic Instructions Before Leaving Earth, so said a Genius. I loved the stories, especially those that depicted the battle between good and evil. I even had a picture Bible at home, and my favorite story was the Temptation of Christ — the one where Jesus faces off against the Devil in the bone-dry desert for 40 days, drier than Canada. God versus the Devil is the ultimate struggle, they are the classic icons of good and evil. The images in my picture Bible were gothic and surreal, the devil depicted as a grinning, burgundy creature with horns, hooves, and a tail. I remember reading a passage and it saying, "Jesus confronts the dragon in the desert, commanding him to get away from him. Satan does as he is told and departs." In the West the dragon symbolized evil incarnate, the devil himself.

The great Swiss psychologist Carl Gustav Jung coined the term "archetypes," powerful images that bubbled up from the collective unconscious. An archetype is an original pattern that continues to exist, and have universal effects on human thinking, imagination, and behavior. Archetypes have transformative power and possibility. The dragon is a powerful archetype.

After school, I would come home, take off my shoes at the door, and my cleanliness-obsessed mother would insist I wash my hands and gargle with salt water every time. Occasionally, we would get Japanese television shows, and I especially loved watching *Kamen Rider*. My Canadian friends had never seen anything like it — Japanese boys transforming into insect motif superheroes who rode motorcycles, epic battles between Light and Dark. It was incredibly cool, and I would often pretend to be one myself. In my imagination, I was Kamen Rider.

On Thursday nights, we would gather to watch *Nippon Mukashi Banashi*, Folktales from Japan, together. The opening sequence featured a song sung by a woman with a hauntingly beautiful voice, listing the titles of famous Japanese fairy tales while images of a little boy riding a dragon, *Tatsu no ko Tarō*, Taro the Dragon Boy, played on the screen. I remember thinking how majestic that dragon looked — benevolent, and not malevolent.

The dragons of the West were so different from the dragons of the East. They seem to mean and symbolize different things. In the West, the dragon symbolized sin, evil, and greed, where the Asian dragon was a symbol for good luck and fortune. The contrast of dragons fascinated me. Why do we love and fear dragons simultaneously? Where do these feelings come from, and what do they truly mean? A mental structure so deeply embedded in human constitution that it manifests itself through the universal image of the dragon.

East and West, both exist at the same time.

Actor's Agency

Ladies and gentlemen, allow me to tell the story of story. The narrative comes first, thus the power of story. After safety, food, and love, children want a story. We yearn for story. It has spiritual, mental priority. From a very young age, children can grasp complex ideas presented as stories when their powers of comprehending the world are still developing. We all see the world in our own unique way, but story is the structure of the way we see our reality. *Story is how we see.*

In Japanese, story is *monogatari*, which combines the words for "spoken" and "things." This reflects how we humans share knowledge and experiences across generations. Speech is something that sets us apart as a species. Imagine a pack of the now-extinct Japanese wolf wandering the landscapes of Honshu. Now, picture that this pack of wolves could engage in conversation. I find this analogy fascinating. Within the pack, the wolves have established a clear hierarchy. When a dominance conflict arises, two wolves confront each other and growl, issuing threats. Yet, rather than resorting to a deadly fight, the wolf that backs down will lie down and expose its neck, a sign of submission. Surprisingly, the winning wolf doesn't go for the kill, instead choosing to show restraint.

This is guided by an unspoken rule, deeply embedded in their instincts: the protection of the pack's weaker members. There is strength in numbers. The next day, when the pack faces a much larger prey, they will need the support of every member. Imagine if one of these self-aware wolves noticed this dynamic and remarked that each wolf in the pack seemed to have inherent worth. The wolves would share a story about it. The shaman wolf would address the gathering pack, saying, "The heroic wolf that spares its opponent's life is a good wolf." This reflects their respect for one another's value. Over time, this story would shape the culture of the pack, forming their own sense of wolf ethics.

We began by observing our own behaviors and creating representations of these patterns, dramatizing them in order to understand the reasons behind our actions as humans. By encapsulating these patterns in stories, we can navigate our daily lives. These narratives guide us on how to behave — what is acceptable and what is not. They serve as a way for us to communicate with ourselves about our actions. A skilled writer captures these observations and presents them in an engaging manner. A powerful story offers a unique perspective on the world and suggests ways we can act within it. Stories equip us with the knowledge we need to survive; they are essential guides to living and navigating our choices. Novels, movies, theater, opera, television dramas, they show us our own possibilities. Then we act them out. *We are all actors*, living out patterns of possibility.

An actor by definition is a participant in a process, but a professional actor embodies a character within a story, becoming a dreamer who brings narratives to life. What a truly honorable profession! That's why we love going to the movies and seeing stories projected on the silver screen. Poof! You're the hero. One gets to be *Burapi* (Brad Pitt) for an hour and a half, doing exciting things. Tristan, a wild, favorite middle-son, well-versed in Native American culture in Ed Zwick's *Legends of the Fall*; Louis, an immortal being with a conscience in Neil Jordan's *Interview with a Vampire*; and Detective Mills chasing John Doe's seven deadly sins and eventually embodying Wrath in David Fincher's *SE7EN*, "What's in the box?" Nothing cooler than Cliff Booth driving in Quentin Tarantino's *Once Upon a Time ... in Hollywood*. Movies have a powerful emotional grip. Filmmakers provide insight into the characters' goals, allowing us to adopt those aspirations and align our feelings with theirs. We begin to understand their emotions, creating a bond that brings us closer. A good actor is like a mirror, reflecting the viewer.

A valuable lesson I learned about film acting happened while shooting the final scene of the Japan-Canada film *The People Garden* (2016) directed by Nadia Litz, where I had the honor of working with the ethereal Dree Hemingway, great-granddaughter of Ernest Hemingway. In the final scene, our characters, Mak and Sweetpea, are sitting in the back of a van, driving away from the haunting Aokigahara Forest also known as the "Sea of Trees" near Mount Fuji. The screenplay aimed for an ambiguous ending that echoed the feel of *The Graduate* (1967). We had filmed it twice, once in the woods of Sooke, BC, and again in a sound studio in Sudbury, Ontario, using a green screen. Clearly, something wasn't clicking. I was trying too hard to achieve perfection and overdoing the performance. As we prepared to shoot the scene for the third time — this time on a road in Shizuoka with the real Mount Fuji looming in the background — I noticed my confidence slipping.

Coincidentally, on the flight to Japan, I had listened to a podcast about the silent film era that featured a story about the iconic actress Greta Garbo. The discussion centered on her final scene in *Queen Christina* (1933), where she gazes into the distance with a stoic yet deeply expressive face. The director had advised her to clear her mind and let go of emotions, allowing her face to become an empty canvas for the audience to project their feelings onto her character. This approach turned the scene into something truly powerful — transforming viewers into co-creators of meaning. As we were about to roll the camera, that podcast anecdote lingered in my mind. Apparently, the director had simply suggested Garbo think about what she had for breakfast that morning. Surprisingly, that mundane thought was enough, and the scene made it into the final cut. Garbo's performance throughout the film had been so well crafted that presenting a blank canvas for the audience's interpretation became the most effective choice.

Embracing neutrality can create the strongest impact, and when achieved, it can shine brilliantly during editing. A skilled actor has the ability to elicit this kind of projection, allowing a performance to embed itself in the audience's subconscious. When I finally watched the completed version of the film for the first time at the Buenos Aires Film Festival, I wasn't shocked to see that the filmmakers had chosen the last take we shot in Japan. Even though I was struggling with a severe case of jet lag after flying in that afternoon, I found myself engaged at the end of the movie. In that final scene, I felt a flicker of optimism from both characters, and the emotional resonance tugged at my heartstrings. (Kate Bush's song *Running Up That Hill (A Deal with God)* helped.) It struck me as remarkable that we had traveled halfway across the globe for that shot. The ambiguous ending was earned, not just for the characters, but for us as actors, making it all the more rewarding. It seems that, as in many myths, the third time truly is the charm.

Stories are woven from threads of imagination, experience, and language. As a child visiting Japan during the summer, I was a budding entomologist, always armed with my insect guidebook and a net, eager to catch creatures of all shapes and colors in the garden. One particular memory stands out: a large cicada landed on the screen door of the house and began to make its loud droning sound. I was determined to add it to my collection, so I called for my Auntie Yoshiko to help me catch it. When she came downstairs and saw the cicada, she immediately said, "That's Grandpa visiting." Oddly enough, that made complete sense to me. It didn't matter anyway because my favorite insect was the *tombo* or dragonfly, with its exquisite design optimized for flight.

Dragonflies have been around since the time of the dinosaurs. I remember gently holding the delicate wings of a dragonfly and dipping the tip of its abdomen into a glass of water to determine its sex. If it was female, she would start releasing a stream of eggs. What's fascinating about dragonflies is that they spend most of their lives in the nymph stage, living beneath the water's surface, where they eat small fish and tadpoles, and breathe through gills. They can remain in this aquatic stage for up to three years. Then, one day, when they're ready to transform, they emerge into the moonlight, climb up a reed, tear themselves apart, and begin their metamorphosis into winged adults.

A dragonfly lives in two distinct phases: as an aquatic predator and then as a master of the air, searching for a mate. Similarly, we also play different roles throughout our lifetime — perhaps as a friend, a loving partner, an actress, or a devoted mother. We inhabit a living theater, each of us a performer with a multitude of characters within, ready to take the stage at a moment's notice — angry, joyful, melancholic, or proud. It is essential that we strive to embody the best versions of ourselves and embrace our roles with purpose. The adult dragonfly lives only a few months, yet its brief existence is filled with energy and vitality. Their life is vibrant but fleeting, mirroring our own short lives. All the more reason for knowing the role we're playing and the kind of story we are part of.

I began my acting career in my teens, participating in productions in both the US and Canada. Starting at thirteen, I became a series regular on a teen drama called *KidZone,* where I played a character named Jai, sharing the same name as my own. This experience taught me an essential lesson: every character I portrayed was a reflection of some part of myself. I learned to be myself, on and off camera. Sarah Chalke and Devon Sawa were co-stars at different times during the run of the show. I also had the opportunity to be a recurring character in *The Odyssey,* a prestige children's fantasy series produced by the CBC, which starred a fourteen-year-old Ryan Reynolds, who is the same age as me. Even back then, he was incredibly talented. A co-star and I often found ourselves lingering after our scenes just to watch Ryan work; his ability to stay in character and improvise at such a young age was remarkable.

I witnessed many peers move on to bigger opportunities — I'll never forget the day we dropped Devon off at the airport for his audition for Spielberg's *Casper*, calling after him, "You're gonna be famous!" It brought a smile to my face when I later saw him as Stan in Eminem's *Stan* music video. During that period, there weren't many audition opportunities for Asian Canadians, *Better Luck Tomorrow.* I made the decision to move to Japan, seeking out more opportunities – not that I was anywhere near as talented as my friends were.

After relocating to Tokyo, I had a brief stint as a VJ at MTV Japan, where highlights included hanging out with Wu-Tang Clan and being serenaded by artists I interviewed before their concerts. *Everything Happens for A Reason*, thank you, Zhané. My time there introduced me to an eclectic mix of artists, each with their own unique perspectives. I recall how each band member answered the same question in completely different ways. Eventually, I connected with an actor's manager who saw potential in me. He assured me that, if I invested some time, he would help me land interesting roles in quality films with reputable directors.

Thanks to his guidance, I began to work consistently as an actor in Japan. Choosing to base myself in Tokyo has significantly influenced my identity as an actor; many of my friends in Japan are photographers, stylists, designers, and actors who were once models, all intertwined with the fashion industry. This environment has made me more aesthetically aware than I might have been had I remained in North America. I can feel my Japanese heritage influencing my behavior – leading me to express emotions through silence, being less verbose, a lot hinging on the small nuances. I feel a strong sense of balance between my two cultures. Acting in a language other than one's first language can open up new emotional avenues and offers a sense of freedom.

As the Japanese scholar and art critic Kazuko Okakura eloquently stated in his work *The Awakening of Japan*, "It's as if the Japanese personified the beautiful mysteries of the world through their dragon *kami* (gods). The Japanese dragon symbolizes both male and female principles, embodying the continuous changes and variations of life, represented by its limitless capacity for adaptation and its ability to thrive in various environments." Truly, the Japanese dragon exemplifies versatility.

The Beauty of Sadness

Children are enchanted with fairy tales because they give children something vital and honest that will stay with them. *Little Red Riding Hood* teaches us to be careful of the Big Bad Wolf; there are malevolent people out there, one might get eaten. There's a darkness at the heart of all great fairy tales. Fairy tales are more than true, not because they tell us dragons exist, but because they tell us dragons can be beaten.

The Japanese psyche is in its fairy tales and one of the most famous is *Tsuru no Ongaeshi*, or "The Crane Wife," a story about how one must make sacrifices in a relationship. In the tale, a young man saves a crane that is trapped and sets it free. Shortly after, he meets a beautiful woman, falls in love, and they marry. To help support their household, his wife offers to weave exquisite silk garments to sell in the market — on the condition that he never watches her while she works. This bargain highlights an important theme: when someone does something kind for us, we often feel the urge to repay them, even if it requires sacrifice. It's a beautiful expression of love and gratitude.

However, the young man's curiosity gets the better of him. Despite being told not to look, he eventually peeks into the room where his wife is working, drawn by an irresistible urge. What he discovers is shocking: his wife, the crane he saved, is plucking feathers from her own body and weaving them into the loom to create the beautiful silk. This moment encapsulates our inherent human curiosity and tendency to break promises, reminding us that even with the best intentions, we can sometimes overlook the sacrifices made by those we love.

The crane wife symbolizes rebirth and transformation. She selflessly sacrifices herself to save her husband, and this act of love allows her to transform into a human and connect more deeply with the world around her. However, once the man discovers her secret, he urges her to stop. She explains that she's been doing it all out of love for both of them. He insists that love shouldn't require sacrifice, but he is mistaken. A person who doesn't make sacrifices for someone they care about doesn't deserve to be with a crane.

In Japan, the crane is a spiritual symbol, famously represented by the red Japan Airlines logo on the tails of their jets. The crane's elegant form in flight also represents the ideal of feminine beauty. After her secret is revealed, the crane can no longer stay and ultimately flies away, never to return. *The Crane Wife* teaches us that if we break trust, lie, or stray from the right path, we risk losing everything we've built. It reminds us to value what we have and not take it for granted, or we might lose it forever. A cautionary tale on the temptations and repercussions of infidelity perhaps. Ultimately, *The Crane Wife* is a timeless story that beautifully illustrates the themes of love, sacrifice, and gratitude.

As an actor preparing for a role, I often draw from my own life experiences, to connect with the character's emotional journey, striving for authenticity in my performance. However, there are times when the opposite happens — if one is fortunate, one might take on a character that isn't tied to one's own experiences, and the process of making the film can transform one's self in unexpected ways.

In 2007, I traveled to Yakushima, an island of breathtaking natural beauty with its ancient, moss-covered forests, to shoot the short film *Tengu Gaiden*, which is an adaptation of the classic story *The Crane Wife*. Part of the Ryukyu Archipelago, Yakushima is a UNESCO World Heritage Site and served as an inspiration for the stunning landscapes in two of my favorite Studio Ghibli films: Miyazaki Hayao's *Nausicaä of the Valley of the Wind* and *Princess Mononoke*. I was excited to discover that our cinematographer was Yoshitaka Sakamoto, a six-time nominee for the Japan Academy Awards, known for his work on one of my favorite Japanese films, *Kamikaze Taxi* (1995). With an incredibly talented director and the stunning backdrop of Yakushima for our story, I felt confident that we would beautifully capture the essence of the tale.

I was cast as Louis, a knight from the Crusades who becomes shipwrecked on an island. After rescuing a beautiful blue crane, he encounters the enigmatic Princess Amaya, portrayed by Kuriyama Chiaki. The director cleverly wove in the Wind God, a beloved mythical creature in Japan, known as the *Tengu*. Tengu are depicted as red beings with large noses, capable of running and jumping faster than anyone else. They wear wooden sandals with a single tooth and carry large feather fans, preferring a solitary life in the mountains. Apparently, foreigners were often mistaken for the Tengu due to their height and prominent noses, with the red skin possibly representing a sunburned Caucasian. Tengu masks, known for their mischievous and erotic attributes, can be found throughout Japan.

I was genuinely excited to work with Ms. Kuriyama. Quentin Tarantino had cast her as the iconic Gogo Yubari in *Kill Bill Vol. 1* after discovering her performances as the lead in the classic Japanese horror hits *Ju-on* and *Battle Royale.* I knew she was a formidable screen presence. I later recalled that when I was 20 and visiting Japan in the summer of 1997, I had seen a photobook at a bookstore called *Shinwa-shōjo,* "Girl of Myth," featuring a very young and demure looking Kuriyama Chiaki in a bathing suit on the cover. At that time, the "Lolita complex" or *lolicon* culture had taken hold in Japan, with a rising demand for younger-looking talent. It was a visually striking photobook and I remember thinking how I'd never seen anything like it before, especially in the West. *Girl of Myth* was my first impression of Chiaki.

Since my character was a shipwrecked knight, I decided to lose weight for the role. By the time we began filming, I was consuming only liquids, mainly black coffee and a concoction of water, lemon juice, maple syrup, and cayenne pepper, the latter supposedly intended to suppress hunger (it did not). I was already slender, so one can imagine how slight I looked —

perhaps that visual contrast with the delicate Chiaki played well on screen. The first scene we shot involved me running down the shoreline while wearing actual chain mail armor, and I almost fainted from exhaustion. My body gave out; I could barely run because I hadn't eaten. If one watches the film, there's a slow-motion shot from behind that isn't me — I was off-camera pleading for some chocolate to raise my blood sugar while watching a young production assistant don a wig and effortlessly leap over a log. It was a humbling moment, and I was grateful for the help.

Mickey Curtis, known as the godfather of rockabilly in Japan, played a mysterious monk in the film. With parents of both Japanese and British heritage, he started his career performing for wounded American soldiers and touring US base camps in Japan after World War II. In 1966, he formed the band "Mickey Curtis & The Samurai," which gained a huge following in Europe. Besides being a great musician, Mickey carved out an impressive acting career and in 1996 he won the 69th Kinema Junpo Award for Best Supporting Actor for his role as a yakuza boss in *Kamikaze Taxi*. On our last night during dinner, Mickey encouraged me to get up and give a speech, saying it was one of the responsibilities that come with being the lead actor on a project.

The whole cast and crew were enjoying some beer and *saké*, reminiscing; it had been an exhilarating film shoot. Throughout the evening, Chiaki and I exchanged glances, we had enjoyed the experience of filming together. It felt bittersweet knowing it was all coming to an end — though I still had one more day of work, Chiaki was set to fly back to Tokyo the next morning. During the week, I had caught wind from her manager that I was Chiaki's type, and had reciprocated the message. As the night wore on, Chiaki and her manager said their goodnights and left since they had an early start. After chatting with a few others and finishing my drink, I excused myself and headed to my room.

My room happened to be on the same floor as Chiaki's, and as I walked down the hall, I noticed an open door a few rooms down. Was this an inviting signal? My adventurous spirit took over, and without hesitating, I walked past my own room to the open door, knocking gently. To my delight, Chiaki appeared, smiling and sans manager. I asked if she'd like to join me for a nightcap in my room, and she agreed. We relaxed in our yukatas, sipping saké and sharing laughter late into the night. At one point, we decided to step outside for some fresh air and take a walk.

We hiked up a small mountain trail that led to the set of the "forbidden chamber," where Princess Ayama's outdoor lair and private bedroom were located. Some trees on the island were over a thousand years old, creating a stunning backdrop that intertwined naturally with the production designer's enchanting set. In our retelling of the fairy tale, Amaya promised to spend her days with Louis but would vanish up the mountain every night, only returning in the morning. She made it clear that he was not to follow her, and if he could keep this promise, they would marry in three years. But a seed of jealousy is planted and begins to drive him mad. The next day, I was set to film Louis' desperate climb up the mountain as he sought to discover where Princess Amaya spent her nights, just as the deadline of three years loomed. I thought to myself, just one more day, Louis!

In many Japanese tales, there's a recurring theme where a woman must vanish when a man looks into a forbidden chamber. This motif is intriguing because the emphasis isn't on the man's guilt for breaking the taboo; instead, it highlights the woman's shame at being seen exposed. As she disappears, her true nature, that of a crane, is unveiled. Meaning the woman cannot live with the man who comes to know her true nature, the naked truth. In order for them to live together as a couple, she has to master the art of concealing her identity.

That night, there was a rabbit in the moon. We made our way to a clearing near the top, where the view was absolutely breathtaking. Just then, the rain began to fall, and we found ourselves kissing passionately. In that moment, we tapped into a spiritual strength that embodies mystical experiences. Maybe it was Chiaki's incredible kindness and beauty, our undeniable chemistry, the enchanting energy of Yakushima, or the timeless story we were living out during our work that day, but I started to lose myself in a Sea of Love, and time seemed to stretch. My ego felt like a deck of cards caught in the wind, dissolving into nothing. I was no longer Jai West making out with Gogo Yubari; I was fully immersed in the experience itself.

Initially, I felt a deep connection with her, and then it expanded to the very ground beneath us. Every blade of grass became an extension of my being, and soon I felt united with the entire mountain, the island, the world — eventually the whole universe. Uni-verse, one song. *Unus mundus*. I realized our interconnectedness, that my existence transcended my birth and would continue beyond death — not as a name or a profession, but as pure consciousness. While my ego had faded away, a sense of the experiencer remained, a pure subjectivity that enveloped me in peace. Just then, the rain ceased, revealing the soft glow of red dawn.

In a few hours, Chiaki would board a plane and leave the island, while I would return to the exact spot where we stood to film the final scene of our story — Louis, alone and contemplating what had gone wrong with the Crane Princess now gone. The main difference between European fairy tales and Japanese fairy tales, are the endings. The Japanese ending is a beautiful ending and not a happy ending. The Japanese fairy tales have melancholic endings, they are tragedies. The heroine in the West is rescued by a splendid man and marries him and they live happily ever after, whereas the heroine of the Japanese tale leaves the man alone and vanishes.

A beautiful woman that just vanishes leaves a deep feeling of sorrow and symbolizes completeness in the aesthetic dimension. Beauty is complete only when feelings of sorrow accompany it. In Japanese fairy tales, the element of beauty is central to the narrative. It's like a garden that, while lovely, bears the burden of fallen leaves. This notion of beauty embraces imperfections and the necessity of knowing the dark side of the feminine. It teaches us that true beauty requires an acceptance of death and loss.

When I returned to Tokyo, everything felt surreal. Chiaki and I lived in the same neighborhood and we met once. I was living with a girl at the time, in a relationship that was spiraling downward towards its end. One day I was out on a walk with my then-girlfriend when I spotted Chiaki up ahead walking with a young man towards us. From my recollection, we both pretended we didn't know each other as we passed by, each accompanied by our significant other. It was a poignant moment, and in that instant, I realized I would never see Chiaki again.

The Precious Pearl

Japanese Noh theater is the oldest form of poetic drama still performed today. Its solemn and formal style presents a captivating display of ethereal beauty that transcends time and space. The French poet Paul Claudel, brother of sculptor Camille Claudel, likened Noh to a moving sculpture, with its staging embodying the eternal. While Noh is often considered an art of symbolic expression, it is grounded in realism, which forms the foundation for its portrayals of deep human emotions.

This art form was originally developed by the renowned playwright and actor Zeami Motokiyo. The term "Noh," meaning "skill" or "craft," sets it apart from the more sensational and comedic Kabuki theater of its time, as it blends poetry, music, and dance to express the ideal of beauty known as *yūgen*. The idea of yūgen is a suggestive, half-revealed beauty that is both elusive and deeply meaningful, often tinged with a sense of wistful sadness. In Japanese poetic aesthetics, yūgen refers to the deep and unknowable aspects of life, infused with an elegance that resonates with the pathos of our existence.

Zeami understood that Noh performance unfolds according to a specific progression: "Every phenomenon in the universe develops itself through a certain progression. Even the cry of a bird and the noise of an insect follow this progression." This progression is known as *jo-ha-kyū,* which translates to "beginning/opening," "break/progression," and "rapid/climax." The structure starts with a deliberate slowness, builds in intensity, and culminates in a swift climax. Once this full sequence is completed, the progression begins again.

Following Zeami's teachings, all major forms of Japanese traditional drama incorporate the concept of jo-ha-kyū, from the choice and arrangement of plays across a day, to the composition and pacing of acts within a play, down to the individual actions of the actors. Movements within movements. The playwright carefully considers the rhythmic and narrative structure of the plot, organizing it according to the principle of jo-ha-kyū. The play starts off slowly, with a gradual unfolding of events, sometimes the actors themselves even move slowly, drawing out every action and every movement into a glacial pantomime. As tension builds, the actions become quicker and more intentional. With each plot development, the pace accelerates, culminating in a final climactic moment, which is followed by a brief denouement.

This structured approach — a slow buildup, an acceleration, and a swift conclusion — defines Noh's unique temporal essence and helps the audience navigate the play, even without a script. By observing Noh within the schema of jo-ha-kyū, the lead-up to the peaks of loudness and speedy movement and beautiful dance fit together with a sense of purpose. Rather than a sequence of plot points, Noh resembles a series of waterfalls, flowing gracefully into each moment and the next.

The Noh actor Yoshi Oida discusses jo-ha-kyū in his book *The Invisible Actor*. He explains that while the forward progression of time may sometimes slow down or become almost imperceptible, jo-ha-kyū still unfolds internally. This can happen through the actor's breath or the beating of their heart. From that momentary pause, the progression starts to develop again, increasing in speed and eventually crashing over the audience like a wave. More importantly, this internal development of time occurs not only from the performer's perspective but also from that of the audience. Oida states, "Since the pattern also exists within the body of the onlooker, the audience experiences a sense of organic 'rightness' when actors use this rhythm. The bodies of the actors and the bodies of the audience become connected, and it feels as if they are sharing the same journey." By attuning to the structure of the piece in this way, audience members can let go of their concerns about the plot unfolding on stage. *Noh is meant to be felt.*

Jo-ha-kyū serves as the foundation for crafting and understanding Noh, and it is through feeling the tempo, cascades, and rhythms of the performance that Noh truly comes to life. By articulating this progression of time, Zeami changed not only Noh Theater but also various other disciplines within the realm of Japanese arts, such as tea ceremony, calligraphy, and swordsmanship. Jo-ha-kyū represents the artistic pattern of introduction, transformation, and impact, which according to Zeami is the rhythmic paradigm of the universe.

The pearl is a precious gemstone created inside an oyster as a defense mechanism against foreign invaders, such as a grain of sand or a parasite that gets into its shell. To protect itself, the oyster secretes layers of crystalline calcium around the irritant, which also forms the iridescent lining of its shell. The process of forming a beautiful, natural pearl takes time, forged quietly in the darkness, born from what is perceived to be a negative intrusion. The oyster endures as it matures the pearl.

The creation of cultured pearls was pioneered in Japan by the Mikimoto Pearl Company, which introduced an irritant into the oysters to create pearls more efficiently and then harvested them. To aid this process, the company trained women to become *Ama*, which translates to "Women of the Sea." These female divers, known for their exceptional skill in pearl diving, were considered superior due to their body composition and ability to hold their breath for long periods. In the 1940s, there were around 6000 working Ama at the height of their popularity, but today, this profession is sadly in decline. Despite the decrease in demand for their unique skills, the enigmatic Ama, often seen clad in white, continue to captivate our imaginations.

The Noh play *Ama* or the "The Pearl Diver," written by Zeami, is a rendition of the Japanese myth of *Tamatori-hime*, "Princess Jewel Taker," a story about a young female pearl diver and a Sea Dragon. The legend begins with a dramatic scene where a Sea Dragon sinks a ship carrying a precious pearl from China to Japan, seizing the treasure for itself. The story then shifts to a small fishing village where a young man meets a beautiful pearl diver who supports herself and her ailing mother through her diving work. As their relationship blossoms, she gives birth to their child, only to discover that her lover is the heir to a powerful clan in Japan. Tragedy strikes when the young man's father passes away, and the Emperor of China sends a magnificent pearl as a tribute to honor him. Complicating matters, the emperor is married to the young man's sister, the late lord's daughter. The grieving father cannot find peace because the special pearl has gone missing.

Determined to help, the pearl diver bravely offers to retrieve the lost pearl from the Sea Dragon's lair. Using her wits, she outsmarts the dragon, soothing him to sleep with a lullaby she often sung to her son. However, as she attempts to escape, the dragon awakens, and he, along with his sea guardians — octopi, sharks, and sea urchins — pursue her. In a desperate move, she hides the pearl in a wound in her chest to protect it. Though she reaches her lover and delivers the pearl, she ultimately dies from her injuries. In a poignant end, the Emperor of Japan recognizes her immense sacrifice and honors her legacy by decreeing that all future Empresses of Japan will descend from her line.

In pop culture, one of the most notable Ama is the fictional character Kissy Suzuki, from Ian Fleming's James Bond novel *You Only Live Twice*. She was portrayed by the beautiful Japanese actress Mie Hama in the film, who also starred in the original *King Kong vs. Godzilla* (1963) and was the only Bond Girl to bear his child until the release of *No Time to Die* in 2021. On my 40th birthday, I had the pleasure of enjoying a fantastic rooftop dinner by chef Mama Luli with the company of Cary Joji Fukunaga, the director of *No Time to Die*, and his lovely Venezuelan girlfriend. He's a half Japanese, half Swiss American filmmaker known for his versatility, having directed *Sin Nombre* and *Jane Eyre*, and earning an Emmy for the first season of *True Detective*.

His film *Beasts of No Nation*, which tells the story of child soldiers in Africa, was also the first feature released as a Netflix original film. He shared how he and his cameraman contracted malaria during the shoot. While his cameraman recovered, he was unable to continue working, so Cary took on the cinematography himself. I still vividly recall the powerful shot in the film where blood-soaked leaves slowly desaturate — a testament to his talent for crafting visually striking narratives.

I asked the director, whom his friends called Joji, about his Japanese heritage and how much he identified with it. With humility, he gave a slight bow and said, "*Yoroshiku onegaishimasu*," with a hint of an accent, understandably. It was clear he felt a strong connection to his Japanese roots. He mentioned the subtle differences he observed in communication styles between his American and Japanese family members, particularly the nonverbal cues from his Japanese relatives, something I can attest to. I asked if he ever considered making a film set in Japan. He revealed that he was in the process of writing a romance set in the 1950s about the Ama. The stunning imagery of women diving underwater, with shafts of light filtering down from the surface, had inspired him to research this story. This visual image sparked his creativity and led him to begin writing the screenplay. I find this approach to storytelling truly inspiring.

The pearl is a metaphor for something beautiful, admirable, rare and valuable. In ancient China, "The Precious Pearl" was a euphemism for the clitoris. It's also the name of an extravagant love hotel in Akasaka-Mitsuke, which was run by yakuza member Gucci "Twilight" Tanaka and adult film star Choco Bon Bon during the bubble economy of the 1980s. However, the most treasured pearl is the orbed jewel held tightly in the claws of the Japanese Dragon. This gem, known as the *cintamani,* is a magical wish-fulfilling stone found in Buddhist and Hindu traditions, akin to the philosopher's stone in Western alchemy. It serves as a crystal ball that can see into the future. Why does the dragon guard this precious treasure?

Dragon Ball, created by the late legendary Japanese manga artist Akira Toriyama, has become a global phenomenon, capturing audiences' imagination around the world. As a child I was a fan of Toriyama's first manga series, *Dr. Slump,* but I knew how much more popular *Dragon Ball* was. The series follows the adventures of Goku, a martial artist in search of the seven Dragon Balls, ancient artifacts that, when gathered, can summon a mystical dragon capable of granting any wish. *Dragon Ball* stands as one of the most successful manga and anime series in history.

What makes reading a novel or watching a movie so entertaining? It's not mere escapism. Do we really understand why we flocked to the theaters to see films like *Star Wars, The Matrix, Harry Potter,* or *Kimetsu no Yaiba*? What drives us to spend our money on comic books and movies, aside from appreciating the artistry involved? Is it because they're naturally captivating, or is there something buried deep within our mind that we struggle to grasp? There's definitely something about these stories that strikes a chord with people.

Stories hold a certain value, they offer insights; pearls of wisdom. The connection we feel is a testament to their depth — the more engrossed we are in a story, the more meaning it has for us. The hidden precious pearl of a story is its pattern. It lingers in one's mind long after one has finished a book or left the movie theater. This narrative pattern helps shape our understanding of the world around us. It's like a psychological glue that brings clarity and direction to our lives — whether we realize it or not, we're all living within a story, and it is inside this narrative pattern where agency is formed.

Princess Tamatori stealing Ryūjin's tide jewels, ukiyo-e by Utagawa Kuniyoshi, 1845

2

Order from Chaos

After being banished from Heaven, Susanoo found himself wandering in the province of Izumo, a coastal region in southern Japan. For months and then years, he roamed the area, observing the struggles of mortals. He took up farming and began to understand the destruction his stormy outbursts had caused, filling him with regret.

"This was so much easier when I could just move the dirt with the wind," he mused to himself.

"Now, it's taking days to till this single field. But these mortals wake up every day to move their little piles of earth without complaint. I can at least keep pace with them."

Suddenly, a thunderous roar shattered the quiet. The farmers around him dropped their tools and fled in terror, and Susanoo found himself running alongside them. In the distance loomed a massive creature, a dragon named Orochi, with eight long necks and a colossal scaly body.

Curious, Susanoo asked why no one was standing up to fight the dragon. But the mortals remained huddled in their hiding spots, paralyzed with fear. Orochi prowled through the village, searching for a child to devour. Growling filled the air.

As the screams of the people echoed around him, Susanoo felt a chill of fear grip his heart. He heard the cries of a victim as Orochi flew away, taking someone with him.

Act of Creation

Our brain is made of two hemispheres. Left and right. Right and wrong. Love and hate. Choice and fate. Heaven and Earth. Death and rebirth. Existence in opposition. Forgive the contradictions.

Opposites are interconnected, and recognizing their relationship can lead to a deeper understanding of the mind. We're hardwired to think in duality. Even our faces reflect this duality, featuring two eyes, two nostrils, and two ears, but just one mouth. Maybe because words are like magic. In Japanese mythology, there's an idea called *kotodama,* which combines the words for "spirit" and "word." It suggests that the words we speak carry unique powers capable of transforming the world.

The yin-yang symbol is two dragons: the white dragon, representing order, clutches a black pearl, while the black dragon, symbolizing chaos, holds a white pearl. This signifies that order and chaos are interchangeable; one can seamlessly shift into the other. Imagine being on a first date, and everything's going smoothly — conversation is engaging, she's laughing, everything feels great. When everything feels just right, one is in order. But if one gets a bit too bold and takes a risk with a risqué joke that doesn't land, suddenly everything feels awkward and starts to freeze up. One is thrown into chaos.

There are different degrees of chaos. For instance, one comes home to one's wife, expecting the usual warm greeting with a kiss and a smile, but today she doesn't. That's minor chaos. It's a whole different ballgame if one comes home to find out she wants a divorce or if she's in an unexpected romantic situation with one's brother. That's major chaos. Life can often appear to be progressing smoothly until, out of nowhere, circumstances shift — poof! Everything changes. This could involve one's partner, job, or health. When adversity strikes in any of these areas, one finds oneself thrust into a different state of existence. It's the same world yet nothing feels the same anymore; it's all shrouded in negativity and darkness. One feels lost, uncertain, engulfed in chaos. Recognizing that one is in chaos is essential; it's a vital life lesson.

Being passed over for an audition or a job interview, being disappointed and frustrated, everything seems to fall apart – that's chaos. When facing betrayal from someone one trusts, or worse, when one betrays oneself, that's chaos. Natural disasters – a typhoon, an earthquake – bring their own chaos. Social upheaval, like a revolution or a riot, represents another form of chaos. Catastrophic events such as a nuclear meltdown or a global pandemic plunge us into chaos as well. War is the epitome of chaos. Thus, we find ourselves navigating the delicate balance between order and chaos, two existential states we move through in our lives.

Ultimately, our world is a tapestry of order and chaos, that is the universal human experience. Is one in order, or is one in chaos? Where one is now and where one is going. Is one moving toward a better place or a worse one? That's the essence of a "story." In a way, a story serves as a map for our feelings, acting like a GPS for our emotions, providing an emotional guidance system. Science deals with logic and explains how nature behaves in the objective world around us, while stories delve into the realm of emotion, revealing what's inside us. We all have our own paths to navigate in this world, and it helps to have a sense of direction. Just like old maps that featured illustrations of monsters in uncharted waters, we need to recognize the unknown. Those warnings – "Here be dragons!" – reflect the uncertainty of exploration.

We're nested in story. Even when one shares one's life with someone, it tends to unfold like a story. A song I liked as a kid was, *I Rhyme the World In 80 Days* from half Japanese Canadian rapper Kish's album *Order from Chaos* (1991). "Last stop, it's the motherland... (Yo, Kish, you went to Africa?) Nah, Japan!" I began my journey in Canada, but I've spent more than half my life in Japan. It's ironic that my mother now lives in Victoria, while I'm in Tokyo – a twist neither of us saw coming.

According to legend, Japan was brought into existence by the divine pair, Izanami and Izanagi. These celestial deities descended from the heavens and utilized a jeweled spear to churn the ocean, giving rise to a dragon-shaped archipelago. After admiring their creation, the deities began to reflect on their own existence. It was here that Izanami, the female deity, felt a pang of embarrassment for her lack of something. In contrast, Izanagi, the male deity, appeared blessed with excess. In a compelling union, they decided to come together, merging the emptiness of lack with the fullness of excess. This passionate intertwining spins the cosmos and marks the dawn of a nation that has always achieved harmonious balance between the beauty of this world and that of the world beyond.

As a child growing up in British Columbia, my mother wisely kept me engaged in traditional Japanese activities. I attended Japanese language school every Saturday, where I learned ink brush calligraphy and practiced *soroban* (traditional Japanese abacus). I also trained in *kendō,* the way of the sword, twice a week. One day, a crew from the CBC came to our dōjō to film our kendō club practicing. A few weeks later, I was thrilled to find out that the news story was actually a piece on *Star Wars*, highlighting how Mark Hamill had practiced kendō to prepare for his role as Luke Skywalker. Being the youngest and smallest student, I ended up being featured quite a bit in the segment, and my family cheered every time I appeared on screen. I felt an immense pride knowing that Luke Skywalker studied kendō.

In my early twenties I was naturally drawn to Carl Jung, buying a book of his collected works, *Symbols of Transformation*, but as I began reading, I realized it was beyond my capacity of apprehension. I was an aspiring actor and screenwriter, inspired by Matt Damon and Ben Affleck's story, writing *Good Will Hunting* themselves. I organically gravitated to Joseph Campbell's *The Hero with a Thousand Faces*, and my understanding of the archetypal patterns in storytelling grew.

The Hero's Journey became my new Bible, being indoctrinated by George Lucas' *Star Wars* as a young boy, playing a worn-out VHS tape of *A New Hope* over and over again. Luke looking off into the distance at a two-sun sunset was formidable in my imagination. "Let go your conscious self, and act on instinct," said Obi-Wan to young Luke.

Dr. Jordan B. Peterson is a Canadian clinical psychologist who has taught at Harvard and is Professor Emeritus at the University of Toronto. His book, *Maps of Meaning: The Architecture of Belief*, written decades ago, along with its lecture accompaniment and the "The Psychological Significance of the Biblical Stories" lecture series on YouTube, presents a truly enlightening experience both in content and in delivery. As a captivating thinker and speaker, he's reminiscent of a real-life Robert Langdon — the Harvard symbologist from Dan Brown's *The Da Vinci Code*, a novel that resonated with our fascination for conspiracies and religious myth. With a combination of passion and intellect, the dandy Dr. Peterson has lived an archetypal life, making him inspiring.

Ironically, Dr. Peterson ascended to public prominence not primarily for his mythological insights but rather for his engagement in the political sphere. It was a zeitgeist moment during the infamous animus interview with the formidable Cathy Newman on Channel 4, where Dr. Peterson answers her inquisition with, "In order to think, you have to risk being offensive." I had hoped that he would serve as a bridge between the Left and Right, acting as a mediator who could play devil's advocate for both sides. Ultimately, his most significant contribution lies not in the political domain but the interface between science and religion, where he navigates the complexities of belief and understanding with remarkable clarity. He's one who has helped redefine God, with his brilliant answer to the question "Do you believe in God?" with, "I act as if he exists."

The oldest known written story is the *Enuma Elish,* a Mesopotamian creation myth. Within its ancient verses, the Goddess of Chaos, Tiamat — a formidable sea dragon — emerges as a central figure. This narrative, dating back over 4000 years, tells of Marduk, the King of the Gods, who possesses all-seeing eyes and the power to utter magical words. In a heroic confrontation, Marduk battles Tiamat, ultimately vanquishing her and fashioning the world from her fragmented remains, creating the realm in which humanity resides. King God fights Godzilla of Chaos!

This epic tale is akin to a battle between a divine king and a monstrous embodiment of chaos; Tiamat was the original dragon. God represents the force that confronts the unknown, shaping it into something tangible and creating the world as we know it. This unknown is essentially chaos — an unpredictable realm where anything can happen. However, chaos is also the fertile ground from which all things emerge. It is the source of order, where structure arises from disorder.

When I stand in line at Starbucks, I line up *in order*. When it's my turn, I step to the counter and speak clearly to the barista and *order*. A menu is chaos because there are so many options, so I make sure I specify what I would like. Tall, hot, black coffee, and after a few moments I get my coffee, just the way I wanted. That moment of getting what I want is the feeling of being in order; I'm calm and everything feels in control. In contrast, if I get an iced coffee when I specifically wanted it hot, that creates a small bit of chaos. And if they handed me a *negitoro maki* instead of my coffee, that would be a whole new level of chaos! I would definitely be thrown off if I suddenly received a tuna sushi roll when I was expecting my hot black coffee.

Our consciousness allows us to think, speak, and act, and we are filled with potential for what the future might hold. So, what do I want to create? I need to place my order — think about what I truly desire. If I don't specify what I want, reality won't take form. I have to choose from the menu of chaos. One can't just make a wish and expect it to come true; that's not how life works, God isn't a delivery service. Think of it like making a pizza from scratch. One has to combine the yeast and flour, let the dough rise, and then roll and shape it. One needs to plant seeds, take care of the vegetables and herbs, chop onions and garlic, and mix in some oregano for a tasty tomato sauce. Top it off with mushrooms and green peppers, and don't forget to let the cheese age. In the real world, creating something meaningful requires thoughts, words, and actions — lots of time and hard work.

In the beginning of the Book of Genesis, God divided light from darkness, creating order from chaos. It is the dynamic interplay of order and chaos that creates our world. We are all creators. Each day, we face a vast ocean of possibilities. To truly learn and grow, one needs to willingly engage with the new, confronting chaos and transforming it into order. We are all part of this creative process; it's a fundamental aspect of our existence. Take action to bring order out of chaos. In doing so, one taps into one's own divinity.

Focus Lotus

One is fundamentally a locus of attention so it's useful to know what one wants because one needs to focus on what one wants to create. "What am I focused on? I should be aiming at something Good." The way the world manifests itself to one's self is influenced by what one's focused on in the world.

Consider one's valence. The hedonic tone one signals out into the world. Is one predominantly in a positive mood or a negative mood? Take how two people look at a rainy day. One guy is bitter and resentful about something in his life. He sees the rain and says, "That's just great! Just what I need to make my day even worse!" Another guy thinks, "Isn't the rain refreshing. The plants and grass must be happy today." They are in the exact same external world, the same outer environment but their internal focus couldn't be any more different.

The idiom "Every cloud has a silver lining" surprisingly doesn't have an equivalent in Japanese, despite the language often using nature as a metaphor. When I explain the meaning of "silver lining" to Japanese people, they always light up in immediate understanding and really appreciate it. Positivity is possibility. The proper direction for our endeavors comes from an orientation of hopefulness towards the future as this makes the possibilities limitless. A bit of the old ultra-valence. One needs to shine one's own light to every situation. "I'm dancing and *Singin' in the Rain*." What one chooses to focus on is everything.

In acting school, early lessons emphasize the importance of listening, relaxation, and sense memory — revisiting past experiences through specific sensory details. The colors we see, the flavors we taste, the textures we feel, the sounds we hear, and the scents we smell. One should integrate sensory practices into daily life as mini-meditations, leveraging mindfulness in ordinary moments. For instance, while waiting for an elevator, I might concentrate on the metal ridges of the keys in my pocket or the sensation of my tongue against the back of my teeth. One could pay attention to the muscle tension in one's hamstring from yesterday's run or the sleek surface of one's iPhone. When caught in the rain, is the feeling of raindrops on one's skin warm or cold?

Taking sensory walks allows one to appreciate smells — like lavender in the air — and engage with the surroundings by touching the smooth concrete wall or feeling the soft grass beneath one's feet. It's an invitation to listen to the subtle sounds around us and to revel in the intricate layers of flavor in our food, each bite a reminder of the beauty of presence. By honing in on the sensations within the body — the blood flowing through our veins, the energy pulsing through — we can escape the cycle of incessant thoughts and embrace the moment. This practice creates a deeper sense of aliveness, bridging the gap between the formless and the tangible. Within us lies a stillness; it simply requires our attention. Focusing on our senses opens a path to the sacred, allowing us to fully engage with the richness of our experiential universe. Embrace the knowledge that one is truly experiencing life. I like to focus on finding balance, positioning myself in the space between, right in the center of the yin-yang symbol.

Sono Sion has been a meaningful collaborator and mentor for me; he's often referred to as the *l'enfant terrible* of Japanese cinema. As a young actor, having the creative encouragement of a master storyteller can be life-changing. One of the reasons I love working with the prolific director is that he creates situations and environments that offer the best opportunities for growth. Without even realizing it, you find yourself pushed to your limits, allowing you to expand your skills and abilities.

In the 2005 Japanese coming-of-age crime film *Hazard,* which was primarily filmed in New York, I portray Lee, a high-energy, speed-laced ice cream-selling gangster. Along with my tall and lanky sidekick, Takeda, played by Motoki Fukami, I take a fresh-off-the-boat character named Shin, played by Jo Odagiri, under my wing and show him the ropes of the American dream. A month before we began shooting, Jo, Motoki, Sion, and I had several rehearsals in a Tokyo studio. I arrived in New York early and booked a room at a hostel near Central Park. *An Actor Prepares*. There, I immersed myself in the city — staying out all night, sleeping on a park bench, getting chased by the cops and even accidentally stepping on a homeless man's head. Fortunately, he was fine. By the time the rest of the cast and crew arrived in New York, I had fully embraced the character of Lee.

I recall Sono-san telling me he wanted Lee to be unpredictable — like a firecracker that could explode at any moment. The first day of shooting was a scene where we were robbing a convenience store, and just before the camera rolled, I caught a reflection of myself and suddenly lost my confidence; I didn't look how I had envisioned. Doubts crept in, and I turned to Sono-san, wondering if he could see through me, if I was the right guy for the role. He walked up to me and fixed my hair, put sunglasses on me, and said, "Like Joe Pesci in *Goodfellas*," giving me a little shove. I appreciated the clear direction, and just like that, my confidence returned.

Filmed handheld on super 16 mm, *Hazard* brilliantly captures the restless spirit of rebellious youth with its verisimilitude style. The movie features several long sequences designed to be shot in one continuous take, lasting between 5 to 8 minutes without cuts — an impressive feat that requires a skilled hand to execute. These extended scenes include intricate dialogue, complex choreography, and precise cues, all relying on the cast and crew's trust in one another to hit their marks perfectly.

One memorable one-take scene unfolds on the bustling streets of Queens. In it, the three of us walk and chat for a few blocks before carjacking a passing Cadillac convertible driven by an extra. We leap into the car, brandishing guns, and continue our dialogue as we drive a short distance, eventually stopping in front of a convenience store. We dash inside to rob it at gunpoint, only to have the store owner chase us out, firing a shotgun loaded with blanks. By the time we're about to shoot for the first time, we've put in countless hours of rehearsal that it's muscle memory and now it's time to rock and roll. As the camera starts rolling and Sono-san calls out, "Action!" I feel a mix of excitement and uncertainty about what will unfold next. I have a sense of the scene, but the spontaneity keeps it thrilling.

There was this one time while we were filming a scene when a couple of real drug dealers approached us, trying to sell us some weed. They didn't even notice the small film crew across the street. Since I was the only native English speaker, I managed to talk them out of it on the fly and in character without disrupting the scene, but it could have taken a turn for the worse. In another scene, Fukami was driving over the Williamsburg Bridge while Jo and I were bouncing back and forth in the convertible, with the camera crew in a car alongside us capturing it all. During one of the U-turns to set up for another take, we got into a car accident. Poor Fukami.

Then there was the time Jo cut his hand while punching a mirror for a scene. Without missing a beat, he calmly wrapped his bloody hand in a cloth and went right back to filming as if nothing happened. There was an unforgettable moment when Jim Jarmusch, Jo's favorite director, just happened to walk by our parked car. We rolled down the window to greet him, and he was so nice and wished us luck on the shoot. The point is, on a Sion Sono set, you never know what's going to happen.

In 2019, Sono-san called me up and asked if I'd like to play the gunman leader in his film *Prisoners of the Ghostland* (2021). Years ago, his first English-language project was supposed to be *Lords of Chaos*, a true story about a Norwegian black metal band that was known for committing arson. But ultimately, it was *Prisoners of the Ghostland*, and I ended up spending a few weeks filming in Kyoto with the Japanese crew and a great Hollywood cast, getting to know Nicolas Cage a little along the way. The first time I met Nick, I yelled, "Cocksucker, motherfucker!" right in his face, and he didn't even bat an eye. It was part of a scene where I was welcoming the Hero to Samurai Town.

We had some cold, wet nights where we'd huddle around a stove telling stories, waiting for the geishas and *kunoichi*, female ninjas, to finish their scenes. Behind the scenes, different cultures were colliding, creating a chaotic yet vibrant atmosphere. This was my third time working with Sion, and there always seemed to be an underlying pattern of chaos on his sets. It feels like Sono-san subconsciously thrives in tumultuous circumstances. Nick found that quite intriguing. He's such a fearless actor, and I've always admired him for his boldness. I told him how much I loved it when he unleashed a bit of insanity in his performances, like Stanley Goodspeed in *The Rock*. At first, he thought I was joking and laughed self-consciously, especially since he's been parodied a lot in the US for his over-the-top style. When he realized I was sincere, he lit up and graciously accepted the compliment. "That's high praise," he said.

Nick's acting is so unpredictable; it gives off an illusion of instability, but there's a lot of control behind it. After he finished his scenes, he stayed to watch my close-up and gave me a smile and nod of approval. He met his future wife, Riko, on set, and I couldn't be happier for them. Standing in between the Chaos Actor and the Lord of Chaos was so much fun. There was a lightness of being. A heightened awareness of play and possibility.

Being in between two worlds feels like having one foot in order, where one's in control and knows what to expect, with the other foot planted in the unknown, in chaos, where anything can happen. There's a sense of security and yet one has no idea what's going to happen next. We feel alert and alive because we have to be ready for anything. We have confidence in our abilities, yet we're also venturing into uncharted territory, trying things we've never done before. The flow of information is at its peak.

When one finds the balance between order and chaos, the experience becomes a meaningful challenge and, in that moment, we push ourselves to grow. We have to think on our feet because unpredictability is the only constant. Improvisation becomes an ally; figuring things out on the fly is necessary. It's where the conscious and subconscious merge, where preparation meets mystery. This blend of precision and flexibility creates a kind of tension of opposites that sparks ideas. It's a very physical feeling of an edge inside one's self, digging at the seam, where something new emerges. It's an optimal experience where we're so engaged in what we're doing that we lose track of time and ourselves and, in that process, rediscover who we are. It's the experience of satori, or the state of flow. Like when we play sports or engage in interesting conversation. When we step outside of our comfort zone, we update our skills and expand our boundaries. We discover that we *can* rise to the occasion.

In life, we often find ourselves oscillating between chaos and order. This is essentially what stories teach us: we can navigate through these different states. Participating in this movement voluntarily is where one finds meaning. The moments of tension in between the double dragons are where we grow and get better.

Chameleon Listen

Acting is all about listening and being attentive. It's about using all your senses to uncover the mysteries of reality. When we truly listen, we open ourselves up to new possibilities and free ourselves from conventional limitations.

One of my favorite scenes in *Hazard* features my character, Lee, passionately reciting passages from Walt Whitman's *Leaves of Grass* as I shout it across the East River towards the Manhattan skyline. It's a moment of bonding with Jo's character, Shin, as we take in the breathtaking sunset surrounded by pink and purple hues. Shooting that scene was an incredible experience, and over the years, people have told me how much that moment resonated with them. Our use of Whitman was a delightful surprise; it fit our characters and the story perfectly. That morning, Sono-san and I wandered into a cozy little bookstore. As we browsed, a book caught my eye — it seemed to glow slightly brighter than the others. I pulled it off the shelf, opened it randomly, and my eyes landed on the first sentence: "I sit and look out upon all the sorrows of the world ... I hear secret convulsive sobs from young men at anguish with themselves, remorseful after deeds done." Sono-san approached and smiled, "Whitman, huh?" We were looking for something for Lee to read to Shin to help him learn English, so on a whim, we bought the book.

Discovering that Whitman passage felt like serendipity – a lucky coincidence that added depth to the film. There was always a scene planned for the characters to bond, but it hadn't been written until we were ready to shoot. It lingered in our minds, waiting for the right moment to materialize. This is a reminder of the importance of being aware and open – both to what's planned and what's unexpected. In filmmaking, some of the most memorable moments come from these "happy accidents," which can feel like signs from the universe. It's crucial to remain receptive to subtle hints from both the outside world and our inner thoughts. Noticing what's around us is the first step in creating something new. The answers we seek are often right in front of us; we just need to tune in and listen.

In 2021, there were attempts to cancel the acclaimed director after a Japanese actor living in LA, who had never even met Sono-san, accused him on Twitter/X of exchanging roles for intimate relationships with actresses, all without any evidence. A major tabloid picked up this hearsay and included it in an article about other Japanese film directors accused of similar acts, some of whom had been found guilty. Unfortunately, because Sono-san is the most famous among them, he ended up becoming the focal point of the story. Once a narrative like this takes hold, it can be difficult to shake off. Despite maintaining his innocence, the backlash was swift, and funding for his upcoming Hollywood projects vanished. Those around him began to distance themselves as well.

A few months after the allegations surfaced, a mutual friend of ours invited me to join a small group for dinner after a visit to an Edo-era Museum. It was reassuring to see Sono-san in relatively good spirits despite everything happening around him. Unfortunately, he couldn't stay long, as he had to leave quickly to meet with his lawyer. He was suing the actor and the tabloid magazine for defamation, committed to clearing his name and regaining his reputation.

Not long after, I received a message from Sono-san asking if I'd like to shoot some scenes with him using his iPhone. I agreed, and when he arrived, he was accompanied by Miyoshi, a *kokeshi* doll-like young woman who was a dancer and artist, dedicated to helping restore Sono-san's reputation. It was heartbreaking to see him; he was a shadow of his former self – feeble and much older than his years. It was clear he needed to be creative again, or he felt like he was just fading away.

Sono-san would send me a few scenes, and we'd meet up for coffee and film them. Sometimes with Miyoshi and other friends, while other times it was just the two of us. At first, it was all in good fun; we didn't know where it would lead, but we both felt it had the potential to become something meaningful. He'd come over, and I'd cook for us while we watched Peter Jackson's *The Beatles: Get Back* documentary or chatted about our favorite artists. By the end of our time together, we'd often find ourselves naturally discovering hints or clues about the direction of the story we were telling.

One day, while he was in Hokkaido, he surprised me by sending a hundred-page screenplay titled "Evaporation." Over the course of nearly a year, we worked on filming it. During that time, he was also dealing with the court proceedings related to his defamation case. There were moments when he would suddenly disappear to Okinawa for weeks at a time. I later learned that he was following the advice of a famous fortune teller with celebrity clients, who had told him to head south for a more favorable outcome in his trial, and he took her guidance seriously.

The process of evaporation represents transformation, where a liquid changes into a gas. Halfway through our shoot, I received a cool video message from him explaining the significance of the title. He spoke about death and how it's always others who pass away in our lives — people and animals we grow close to, highlighting the impermanence of their presence. Then, one day, it becomes your turn to leave. He reminded me not to take life for granted. Three years before, he had suffered a heart attack the day after his daughter was born. In his recalled experience of death, he had seen a light at the end of the tunnel. He told me with a smile that going to the other side was really easy and not a hard thing to do.

The final day of shooting took place in his hometown of Toyohashi, where the local film commission had arranged for over a hundred extras, including the mayor. This was just a few days after he won his court case, the verdict was innocent, vindication. The magazine issued an apology and took down the articles. The last shot involved us running through a field we discovered off the highway, chasing the fading light. As dusk settled, he announced that we were officially wrapped after a year of filming. I hugged him and said congratulations. The filming process and the film itself reflected our personal journeys, which made it all the more meaningful to me. It was intertwined with everything happening in our lives. He got better, I got better and the movie got better. We got better together. An experience I will treasure forever. Thank you, sir.

The organic process of Sono Sion's *Evaporation* centered on being attentive to the world around us while making the movie. The creator's role is to recognize what often goes unnoticed. This act of noticing is a creative way to engage with our surroundings. Just like a muscle, attention can be trained, allowing one to develop a unique perspective that highlights what others might overlook. One should embrace the playful exploration of everyday wonders that resonate with one's self. Mastering the art of noticing is essential to any creative endeavor. Go for a city walk and look upward and count how many surveillance cameras one spots. Think different, like Steve Jobs.

One of my longtime friends from high school was an industrial designer at Apple. He and his Japanese wife are close friends with the talented couple Michael Fassbender and Alicia Vikander, and I've had the fortune of spending time with them a few times. My friend met Michael just before he took on the role of Steve Jobs in Danny Boyle's film *Steve Jobs* (2016), and they hit it off immediately. The first time I met them, we went for drinks at a classic rock bar in Shibuya after dinner. When I expressed how much I admired *Shame* (2011) directed by Steve McQueen and Michael's compelling performance in it, Alicia shared an interesting story. While she was filming a movie in New Zealand, her father called her to talk, and he mentioned an intense film he had just watched about a man struggling with sex addiction, highlighting how powerful the lead actor's performance was. Alicia replied that she was currently filming opposite that very actor. It's a funny coincidence, her father had no idea this actor would soon become his son-in-law. Alicia and Michael met while collaborating on Derek Cianfrance's lighthouse romance *The Light Between Oceans* (2016). Their experience during the making of that beautiful love story—both on and off camera—became a lasting memory captured on film, a cherished memento to share with their children about how their parents first came together.

When Michael Fassbender smiles and laughs at something you said, it feels like you have a life. He radiates charisma; it's like the light shines from his face. At that time, he was taking a break from acting to focus on race car driving. He had an upcoming race that he was really excited about, and he even acted it out for me. He's fast around the bend. Race car driving is intense, your life is literally on the line, you're living on the edge. Canadian F1 driver Lance Stroll once shared in an interview that what he loves about racing is the "sudden chaos" that comes with it. It's all about maintaining control in extreme conditions where countless things can go wrong, especially when you're hitting speeds of 220 mph. It's a mix of unpredictability and precision; you rely on your instincts — what Fassy calls "the gut."

We started discussing luck, and I thought of British mentalist Derren Brown's experiment, *The Secret of Luck,* where he created a rumor about a lucky dog statue in a small English village that led to surprising outcomes. We both agreed that luck matters, but most importantly one has the power to create one's own luck, particularly by staying open to possibilities. It was around that moment where I experienced one of those peculiar and meaningful coincidences that Jung referred to as synchronicity. Michael flashed me one of his charming smiles, and suddenly, I recalled that he had portrayed the famous psychologist Carl Gustav Jung in the film *A Dangerous Method,* directed by the renowned Canadian filmmaker David Cronenberg. Coincidentally, I was in the early stages of writing this very book, having spent the day contemplating Jung's concepts and delving into his writings. Here I was, deep in conversation — yin and yang — with "young Jung." This was the essence of synchronicity — a series of anecdotal moments so striking that they demand our attention. These echoes, strange coincidences, serve as reminders. They draw parallels between our inner experiences and the outer world, suggesting something profound about the hidden layers around us.

Staying open to meaning and mystery is the creator way of life, a mode of being in the world. Being aware of one's connectedness to something greater than one's self and having the courage to listen for those subtle whispers is the source of creativity. It's good to give life to what emerges from our unconscious minds and to share it with others. Art plays a crucial role in making our creations endure and serves as a doorway; through the expressions of others, we catch glimpses of the life we're all a part of.

While the world around us is shaped by uncontrollable forces, we have the power to engage in a creative journey within ourselves, uncovering a more authentic and complete identity. One should take a moment to be aware of one's own creativity. Acknowledge, "I'm living this right now. Look at what I've created." Reflect on what's going on, around one's self and within one's self. By stepping back and observing one's thoughts, feelings, and experiences, it becomes a second act of Creation.

Everyone has the potential to shape their own inner world by integrating different aspects of themselves, including both the conscious and unconscious mind. This involves a harmony of opposites — order and chaos, light and dark, good and evil — which leads to a richer understanding of who we are. These opposing elements can coexist within a greater unity, embodying the concept of *coincidentia oppositorum*, the mythical pattern of the coincidence of opposites. This recognition of duality helps us grasp the complexity of the human experience.

Deux Deus Ex Machina. The evening was winding down, and a lovely night was coming to a close. I'll never forget the moment when it was just the three of us left in the bar. Elton John's *Tiny Dancer* was playing, and as I leaned back, I watched Alicia and Michael get up and dance together. I've been around many couples in love before, but what I experienced with those two felt like a scene straight out of a movie. In that moment, I felt invisible. Their love was palpable, and witnessing such pure happiness up close was truly incredible. It was in that moment that I realized the same light I saw in their eyes was mirrored in mine. I was them; I felt their joy.

Morning After Tokyo

In the early spring of 2009, at 33 years old, I was enjoying a moderate level of success as a film actor. I was part of an eclectic cast in the Japanese box office hit *Survive Style 5+* and had appeared in a few high-profile television commercials. I had a leading role in a big summer movie directed by a renowned manga writer that was about to premiere, and I was also featured in a major fashion brand video set to be released.

Additionally, I had just wrapped up a national television and digital advertising campaign in which I co-starred with one of the most popular actresses in Japan. After we finished filming, this wonderful actress, a cultural icon and household name, turned to me and said, "Jai-san, the Japanese people are going to love you!" I was on top of the world.

Intuition and dreams hold great significance. One morning soon after, I woke up in a cold sweat from an extremely vivid nightmare, with just one haunting image lingering in my mind: the fearsome face of the *hannya,* the female demon from Japanese Noh theater. Noh is an art form known for its use of masks, and the hannya is one of its most iconic. This mask represents resentment and depicts a woman on the edge of madness, consumed by jealousy and driven by a desire for revenge against the world.

I was quite familiar with this image; my mother had a white hannya mask hanging on our wall when I was growing up, and it always terrified me. The hannya mask is both demonic and dangerous, yet when viewed from a different angle, it can also convey sorrow and torment, showcasing the complexity of human emotions. When an actor looks straight ahead, the mask appears frightening and angry, but when tilted slightly down, it seems to express deep sadness, almost as if it's crying. With subtle movements the actor has the ability to change the expression of the mask. It is up to the performer to imbue the mask with emotion.

That morning, after waking from the nightmare, I immediately started writing the dream down. I was used to doing my Morning Pages, a technique I learned from Julia Cameron's *The Artist's Way*. The idea is to write one's stream of consciousness as soon as one wakes up, without stopping until one has filled a few pages. I swear by the power of Morning Pages; like drops of clear water into a muddy glass, they help clear away the clutter of unnecessary thoughts in the subconscious mind, leading to a surge of useful ideas. It's a tried-and-true method for tapping into a vast reservoir of creativity. I was writing furiously, hoping to capture my thoughts before they slipped away. What did the dream mean? What did the hannya symbolize? Was it some kind of premonition? Suddenly, right in the middle of my writing, at precisely 8 a.m., a dozen police officers burst through my door, raiding my small apartment.

The two police detectives wore smirks on their faces.

"Mr. West, you're Beethoven from the Tokyo Gas commercials, right?" one of them asked. I nodded in response.

"We're pretty sharp, aren't we?" said the lead detective as they sat me down, making it clear not to move. I was surrounded as they began rifling through my tiny apartment, which only highlighted just how many officers there were.

"Don't you have bigger fish to fry?" I asked. One of them conducted a chemical test on a small bud they'd found in an empty coffee can. I told them what it was, insisting that the test wasn't necessary. Moments later, the plant turned blue.

"This is *taima* (cannabis!)," he announced with pride.

I was arrested for possession of 0.2 grams of cannabis. It turned out they were following a lead, they had intercepted a package that my then 56-year-old hippie half-sister in Vancouver, an avid medical marijuana advocate, had sent me. An unexpected gift, a late Christmas care package full of baked goods, that included her specialty, edible marijuana cookies.

They escorted me out onto the street, handcuffed, and into a police car. It was beyond humiliating. I was on the verge of realizing all my dreams when, and in an instant, I lost everything. My life as I knew it was completely turned upside down — and it was all my own undoing.

3

Susanoo's Sacrifice

The villagers went back to their farming, choosing to overlook the sorrow of a family mourning another lost child. Susanoo felt a mix of confusion and fear, unsure of why the villagers accepted their fate so easily. Despite his turmoil, life continued around him. He worked the fields, rested, and each year, he avoided Orochi whenever it came to feast. After ten long years of being shunned, Amaterasu showed him no signs of forgiveness, and he grew weary of running from the serpent. These villagers were his friends, his responsibility, and he knew it was time to step up and protect them.

One day, he approached a small castle filled with tears, where an elderly couple cried beside their young daughter. The old man spoke, his voice heavy with despair: "Every year, this eight-headed serpent comes to claim one of our daughters. It has taken seven, and soon it will demand our last, Kushi-inada-hime." Moved by their suffering and captivated by the beauty of the girl, Susanoo offered a deal: he would confront the dragon if they would give him Kushi-inada-hime's hand in marriage. Faced with the grim reality of their situation, the old couple agreed without hesitation. To protect her, Susanoo transformed Kushi-inada-hime into a comb and tucked her safely in his hair.

Mythological Underworld

They asked me whether I wanted to go to *gaijin* (foreigner) jail or Japanese jail, and I chose the latter. By the time I was finally finished with the processing, it was dark outside. As they brought me in, handcuffed, the head guard let me know reassuringly that newspapers wouldn't be made available the next day. In a daze, I simply nodded and said, "*Arigato*."

As we walked toward the cell area, a sudden fistfight broke out right in front of me. A half Brazilian albino *chinpira* (yakuza punk) tried to jump me, but a massive yakuza stepped in to protect me. It was a burst of violence right from the start. The first night in jail was overwhelming, filled with pure fear and anxiety. Surrounded by the unknown, the reality of my situation began to sink in as I felt the walls closing in. In my naive foolishness, I still held onto the hope that once morning came, I could explain myself and maybe get away with everything unscathed. Meanwhile, my four cellmates snored all night long, but I couldn't sleep a wink.

Dreams can reveal the story one is living. When we understand our story, we gain psychological wisdom and are better equipped to find meaning in our lives. Dreams present visions of what's possible, and when someone can grasp that vision and share it, others can help bring it to life. Dreams are the seeds of myths, bubbling up from our subconscious minds. Stories we created over thousands of years in an attempt to formulate what guides us and to transmit the knowledge forward. If one wants to explore the depths of reality, understanding myths is essential.

The most memorable stories are the ones that get retold. The best stories become mythology and religious stories. Myths are unforgettable, yet hard to understand. We shouldn't take them literally but understand them symbolically. They are truthful lies. Did these stories really happen? They did, but in a way that resonates on a deeper level, a truth that continues to unfold.

The *Kojiki,* "Records of Ancient Matters," was compiled at the request of Empress Genmei after she ascended to the Chrysanthemum Throne. It was designed to create a narrative that justifies the rule of the House of Yamato through myth and legend, showcasing the heavenly deities and their rightful heir to the land of Japan. Along with the *Nihon Shoki,* "The Chronicles of Japan," these two texts serve as a compilation of Japanese creation myths, ancient legends, hymns, and oral traditions that describe the origins of Japan, its kami (gods), and Imperial lineage. Together, they form a unified "official" mythology, giving Japan its identity.

Imagine gathering the most popular stories of all the gods from various tribes across Japan, from the Ainu of Hokkaido to the Ryukyu people of Okinawa, and distilling the common patterns from those tales into one book. It's like taking the ten best stories and condensing them into a single volume, creating distilled gods much like fine *shōchū* (Japanese vodka) — capturing the very essence of these ultimate deities.

The narratives that made it into the *Kojiki* and *Nihon Shoki* are rich in wisdom. For example, Susanoo, the Storm God, is a fascinating figure. He embodies a mix of good and evil, presenting a complex character. He can be seen as either a wild and impulsive god of the seas and storms, or a heroic figure. Susanoo's mischievous actions eventually led to his exile from Heaven, leaving him lost and confused, wandering in the mythological underworld. This is where one ends up when things fall apart. If one knows that's what that means, one has one of the keys that opens up ancient stories to one's self.

Bathing day in jail happened every five days, and I happened to arrive just after it had taken place. Imagine five days of sweat, grime, and fear caked onto your skin from head to toe before finally getting the chance to wash off. I sat down at the only empty stall and was about to turn on the water when I heard a grunt behind me. In the tiny, moldy mirror, I caught a glimpse of the half Brazilian albino yakuza punk, clearly annoyed that I had taken his spot. I quickly realized my mistake, but I was too exhausted to move.

Then, the yakuza boss — covered in a full body cherry blossoms tattoo — sitting at the farthest stall turned around and shouted at the punk, telling him to scrub my back and let me use his stall. The chinpira apologized, bowed, and started scrubbing my back with a towel that was so rough it felt like I was being cleaned with a steel sponge. I thought I was about to get my ass kicked, but instead, I ended up experiencing VIP treatment.

The Japanese live to bathe and wash themselves thoroughly before boiling themselves in searingly hot communal baths. We cook ourselves at moments of crisis in order to transform ourselves from natural beings to social beings. I submerged my fatigue-soaked body into the dark brown hot water. To this day, the best sensorial experience I've had was immersing into that first bath I had in almost a week. My bath with the yakuza felt so fu*king good.

My lawyer, Kobayashi, who was sent to me by an actor friend Prada, told me that I would be held for thirty days. After that, if I paid a bond of three million yen, I could be released. One of the hardest moments for me was seeing my manager, a man who had dedicated his life to nurturing actors, sitting across from me behind a plate of glass, flipping through a binder filled with newspaper clippings and printed Internet articles about my arrest. He broke down in tears, and we both cried, overwhelmed by the weight of my betrayal. It was a heavy burden for both of us to carry.

Naturally, all my film and commercial projects were put on hold or cancelled immediately. I had violated the cardinal rule of show business: once a project is completed, don't do anything stupid. My interesting interactive website was deactivated, my YouTube channel deleted by my agency. I felt like I had let so many people down, and the weight of it crushed my soul. I became the living embodiment of the Icarus myth, the story of a boy who flew too close to the sun and lost his wings, a tale about hubris and pride.

For the next week, I faced interrogations by police detectives as I desperately tried to convince them of the existence of my 56-year-old half-sister Maria. They believed she was a figment of my imagination. In the package she sent me, there were several business cards featuring her name, "Maria West," along with her glamorous headshot — a picture of a smiling middle-aged Caucasian woman. The police, however, believed the cards were fake and thought that "Maria" was simply code for marijuana. Eventually, we proved her existence with a video message from her, but the damage had already been done.

My guilt and shame spiraled into a deep unhappiness and depression over the following weeks. I had become the very type of person I once looked down upon — a bitter hater. I channeled my resentment into writing an essay in Japanese addressed to the Prosecutor, pleading for the chance to continue my acting career in Japan. I witnessed firsthand what it was like to lose my vocation, to not be able to do what I love to do; I feared my heart would never fully recover if I couldn't act again. For me it was like I was holding onto a candle and safeguarding the small flame in the cold and windy night, making sure it doesn't go out. In the essay I described my sister's lifestyle in Vancouver and the culture she was immersed in, in which the young prosecutor responded, "As if medical marijuana is such a thing!"

The first question a fellow inmate asks is, "What are you in for?" I quickly realized I was the only one inside for marijuana. Most of the people were there for *shabu*. Japan's a speed culture, methamphetamines have long been the Japanese drug of choice. This drug was introduced to the Japanese military by pharmaceutical companies, particularly during the late 1930s and throughout the war years, to keep soldiers awake and combat fatigue, enhancing their alertness and endurance. I also remember seeing an inmate who was a medical doctor who appeared regularly on TV, who ended up in prison for fraud, and he seemed really depressed.

One day, deep in my despair, a guard came to my cell with a handwritten letter from a fellow inmate a few cells away. It was from the massive yakuza who had stepped in to break up the fight and protect me without hesitation on my first day. The letter was surprisingly eloquent, written in English, filled with warm words of encouragement urging me not to give up. It brought me to tears because it was exactly what I needed. At first, he terrified me. He was enormous, and I found his battle-scarred face intimidating. But as I got to know him better, I was surprised to realize how young and wise beyond his years he was. He was in jail for armed robbery and had been stuck in the system for over a year, waiting for a court date due to complications with the case and others involved. His fellow robbers had different stories. He ran a *herusu*, a brothel, with his new bride whom he missed dearly, and he had a child with another on the way.

He asked the guards to transfer me to his cell so he could practice his English, but I politely declined. Instead, he would come by my cell to visit whenever he could. His smile brightened my day; he was purer than I could ever be. This became a comforting routine — receiving letters from the gentle giant, notes passed from cell to cell until I got them. He became my unlikely new friend. I still have his letters, and they continue to inspire. The one I thought was most threatening ended up being the one who helped me get through my toughest times — never judge a book by its cover.

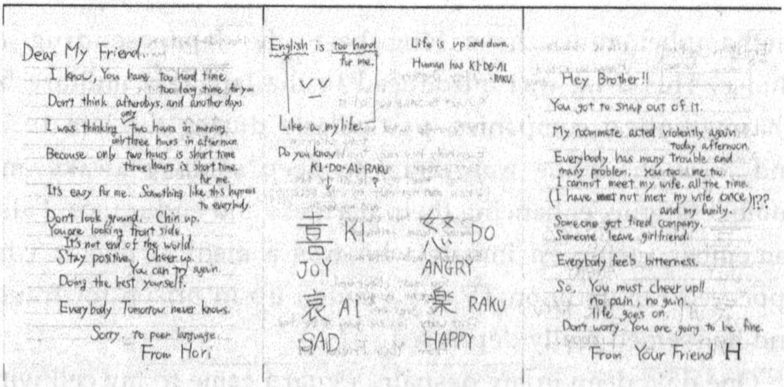

Dear My Friend.
I know, You have too hard time
two long time for you
Don't think afterdays, and another days
I was thinking only two hours in morning
only three hours in afternoon
Becouse only two hours is short time
three hours is short time.
for me.
It's easy for me. Something like this happens
to everybody.
Don't look ground. Chin up.
You are looking front side.
It's not end of the world.
Stay positive. Cheer up.
You can try again.
Doing the best yourself.
Everybody Tomorrow never knows.
Sorry. to poor language.
From Hori

English is too hard for me.
Like a my life.
Life is up and down.
Human has KI-DO-AI-RAKU
Do you know KI-DO-AI-RAKU ?
喜 KI
JOY
怒 DO
ANGRY
哀 AI
SAD
楽 RAKU
HAPPY

Hey Brother!!
You got to snap out of it.
My roommate acted violently again
today afternoon.
Everybody has many trouble and
many problem. You too. me too.
I cannot meet my wife. all the time.
(I have not met my wife once)!?? and my family.
Someone got fired company.
Someone leave girlfriend.
Everybody feels bitterness.
So, You must cheer up!!
no pain, no gain.
life goes on.
Don't worry. You are going to be fine.
From Your Friend H

Letters from a yakuza, 2009

What does one do once in the underworld, especially when one knows one played a role in getting there? It can be a confusing place. The journey into the underworld symbolizes a loss of direction within ourselves. Like the sundial at night that loses its meaning, when we find ourselves in the dark, we are left with the vastness of eternity.

This descent is an essential part of the process; we have to navigate through this darkness, as there's no avoiding the abyss along the way. What's looming in front of us is likely what we'd rather not face. When one finds oneself entrenched in chaos and recognizes that it's one's doing, that acknowledgment can be the hardest part. Entering the underworld means delving into the hidden aspects of one's psyche, exploring the unconscious mind. It's a path of self-discovery, where one engages with archetypes. Magic often unfolds in these deepest, darkest moments of our journey. The suffering we endure becomes necessary for us to find meaning.

This fall makes us reflect on our actions: it prompts us to consider what went wrong. In Japanese, this concept is known as *hansei*, self-reflection. The true power of this process lies in posing the right questions: Where did I go astray? What can I do to make it right? How can I improve myself? Suffering opens the path to deep questions. One should keep refining those questions — it takes time to get clarity.

Life Is a Film

For the Noh theater actor, donning a mask is akin to the art of makeup — it is a transformative experience. Noh performers believe that these character masks embody a profound power that transcends mere appearance, imbuing the act of performance with a spiritual essence. We all put on masks in life. The great tragedy is when the mask becomes you.

The small eye openings in the Noh masks limit the actor's field of vision, adding a layer of challenge to their craft. On every corner of the Noh stage there are columns to help guide the actor but he must also picture himself just from the audience's perspective to really understand his positioning. This practice demands the ability to honestly assess oneself from a detached perspective.

It is no easy feat to observe oneself with objectivity. True humility involves a clear recognition of one's own shortcomings. An actor deeply versed in Noh art understands their own areas for improvement, acknowledging their frailties as essential to their growth. Much like cultivating a *bonsai,* one must examine their development from multiple angles and perspectives. Embracing the mindset of "I don't know what I know" exemplifies genuine humility. After all, not everything is as it appears. When one becomes aware of the vastness of their ignorance, they open themselves to learning and growth, becoming attuned to the nuances of their craft.

My time in the Japanese jail happened to coincide with the peak blooming of the *sakura*. There was a small window in my cell that was slightly open, and if I leaned against the wall and tilted my head just right, I could see a cherry blossom tree in the distance across the courtyard. Those brief moments of seeing the delicate pink petals became a source of solace amid the dreary routine, giving new meaning to the tradition of *hanami*.

Literally meaning "see flower," hanami is the custom of enjoying the beauty of cherry blossoms while having a picnic and sipping saké beneath the blooming trees. This springtime tradition embodies the Japanese aesthetic known as *wabi-sabi*. This concept celebrates the beauty found in imperfection, impermanence, and incompleteness, encouraging us to appreciate the transient, the humble, and the unconventional elements of life. Like a touch of *wasabi*, it's the slight discomfort that often brings out the beauty.

Time seems to move slowly when one is confined to a cell for most of the day. The bleakness of my circumstances began to weigh heavily on my mind. During those moments of reflection, I experienced a sense of inner separation between my anxious, depressed self, and a deeper, more essential aspect of my being — my consciousness. It became clear to me that this unhappy version of myself was not truly real; I had been identifying with my negative thoughts and crafting a self-made story. The past and the future exist only as illusions in our minds, filled with regret and fear.

The present moment is so fleeting that we often can't inhabit it, leading us to retreat into our stories instead. Self-reflection allows us to step away from the immediacy of the now, as we imagine past and future scenarios that we end up tormenting ourselves with. In confinement, however, I was forced to confront the present moment directly, with no distractions to escape into. When the past and future were stripped away, leaving only the present, something within me began to transform. Inside that cell, I was able to dis-identify from my unhappy self and observe it from a distance. This shift took me from the painful cycle of negative self-talk to a heightened awareness of the now. Ultimately, I came to realize that my suffering stemmed not from my situation, but from the mental narrative I held about it.

Life can be likened to a film. We all know that sense of anticipation when we settle into a darkened movie theater — although with the advent of streaming perhaps not so much these days. The flickering light, as images dance across the silver screen telling epic tales of adventure and romance, stirs deep emotions within us. We've all been so engrossed in a movie that we completely lose awareness of our surroundings, wrapped up in the plot to the point where there's no recognition of sitting in a theater. However, it's also possible to be fully immersed in the film while maintaining a background awareness of our environment, a recognition that we are sitting inside a movie theater. This is what meta-awareness — or mindfulness — entails: knowing that we are thinking. "These are just thoughts. They do not define me." It involves taking a calm and balanced perspective toward the ebb and flow of our feelings and thoughts, observing them as what they are rather than identifying with them.

Meditation teaches us that our most minimal sense of self often acts as a focal point, a locus of attention that pays attention to each thought as it emerges in our consciousness. Just like our heartbeat or breath, thoughts flow continuously and relentlessly, each vying for our attention with their own stories. "Don't forget me! Remember that time when she rejected you! When you weren't good enough!" We need to treat each thought with care, much like a child who wants to play: we can acknowledge the thought without judgment or reaction, then gently let it go. The thoughts and emotions we encounter are fleeting, and it's important to remember that they are just that — thoughts and emotions — not the essence of who we are. By cultivating this meta-awareness, we can significantly reduce unnecessary suffering. Thoughts and emotions are ephemeral; they are simply passing experiences, not our identity.

Much like a Noh theater actor, it's essential to become both the lead performer and the audience simultaneously, experiencing both perspectives within one's self. Each viewpoint serves as both the subject and the object for the other at the same time. When life feels especially overwhelming, try to take a step back and view it as if one is watching a movie. Imagine one is observing a dramatic scene where the protagonist is oneself, yet somehow not oneself. Consider what will happen next in the story, what actions the hero or heroine will take, and reflect on one's role within this narrative.

In this process, one's thoughts and emotions can feel distant, allowing one to experience them without being fully engulfed. One can maintain this detached perspective whenever one chooses. Pay attention to one's intuition by looking beyond the surface, staying open to what may unfold in a deeper layer of one's mind. Cultivating meta-awareness is vital, though it's often easier said than done. We tend to cling to habits that lead to our own torment. One of the most common forms of this is unnecessary thinking, which we engage in to escape the deep emptiness stemming from our disconnection from nature. This sense of separation comes from our tendency to label and categorize our experiences, which can be especially damaging in our interactions with others. When we meet someone, our minds quickly judge them based on preconceived notions, often leading to negative assessments and a feeling of distance. We even label ourselves, unpleasant as it is to live with an extremely self-critical mind, "Why did I do that? I should have done better." One can become free of that by realizing these are thoughts.

As one wanders through the forest, if he finds himself constantly analyzing and interpreting what he sees, he risks turning his experience into mere concepts. This mental barrier pulls him away from the vitality of nature and the people around him, as everything becomes just abstract ideas. By getting caught up in this cycle of thinking, he has unintentionally isolated himself from the vibrant life that surrounded us. The sensation of disconnection is rooted in the constant labeling that one's mind imposes, including on one's self. This separation is something one creates. Instead, try to experience the forest without those labels. Allow one's self to feel the energy flowing through the trees and embrace the sacred connection that exists between one and nature.

As one engages purely with their senses, the barriers of separation begin to fade, creating a sense of unity where differences become less important. This kind of engagement cultivates compassion, helping one empathize and connect with others on a deeper level. We should practice kindness and goodwill towards those around us, recognizing that we are not entirely separate from one another. When one stops automatically labeling others, true compassion can emerge naturally.

A significant breakthrough occurs when one realizes there's a constant chatter in one's head, and that one could actually be happier and more productive without it. This awareness creates a space where one can observe the thoughts that continually occupy one's mind. My dear friend Imalu once said "the real you" gets to decide which thoughts to focus on, and I find that idea beautiful. What does it feel like to connect with "the real you"? Not just one's physical self or one's past, but a deeper sense of existence — one's core being. Subjectivity. It's what is left when the personal narrative dissolves, just the experiencer, pure, raw subjectivity. It's what we are, what everyone is. Through self-reflection, introspection, and self-inquiry, one can explore what one thinks is one's personal mind in search of its essence. As one does this, one can move beyond one's mind and into a state of Infinite Mind.

When the suffering becomes too much to bear, one transcends mind and becomes one with it. The awareness of thought transcends thought itself; it's like shining a light on a thought. This pure consciousness allows one to recognize that one is the very awareness that sought to understand itself. When the mental noise becomes too much to handle, it collapses, leaving behind only a sense of pure presence and awareness. One may find something within oneself that is deeper than the identity one once held. The individual still exists, but something far more profound shines through.

This is the experience of Oneness — an awareness of being connected to an inner divine presence that resides within us all. It's not about losing oneself; it's about expanding oneself. It's about at-one-ment, atonement — a journey of redemption. I found myself stepping out of the relentless stream of thoughts. One can't free oneself from a prison unless one first realizes one is locked inside.

iGod

About three weeks in, I woke up feeling completely at peace. The dull cell that confined us suddenly felt refreshing and new. The soft light coming in through the small window had a magical quality to it. As I went through my usual morning routine of folding the futon and cleaning the floor, I felt an underlying sense of tranquility that I had previously overlooked. The comforting presence of the cup of tea we received, the faces of my yakuza cellmates, the expressions of the police guards patrolling the cell block — everything seemed so serene.

It felt as though I had passed through the boundaries of my mind, through the doors of perception to the ultimate nature of reality. It was an experience that I had before, the Sea of Love, but this time I could grok it even more clearly; it was an ocean of consciousness. We are all interconnected like a chain of islands, linked at a deeper level. Jung referred to this shared layer of the psyche as the collective unconscious. Our individual lives emerge as visible pods from this eternal, unseen matrix.

In the vast ocean of consciousness, our individual minds are like waves that rise from it. While each wave seems to exist independently, they are all fundamentally composed of the same essence — consciousness. Hindu philosophy, particularly Advaita Vedanta, or nondualism, describes how the Infinite Mind becomes localized into a finite mind where thought and perception emerge. Due to ignorance, we mistakenly identify with our ego, leading us to believe we are separate from Universal Consciousness or Brahman, the Divine.

The wonderfully affable philosopher and computer scientist Dr. Bernardo Kastrup likens our existence to individual whirlpools of mind in the expansive ocean of mind-at-large. He illustrates this by discussing dissociative identity disorder, formerly referred to as multiple personality disorder — similar to the character played by James McAvoy in M. Night Shyamalan's *Split*.

Each alternate-personality represents a disassociation within the patient's mind. We can look at this as a model for the behavior of mind. By examining these mental processes more broadly, we can gain insight into how each of us serves as dissociated aspects of the greater mind-at-large. You and I are like alter-personalities, fragmentations of Universal Mind.

When we fall asleep and start to dream, we dissociate from ourselves and become fully immersed in our dream personas, a common experience that happens every night. A part of our mind disconnects from the rest. Dreams serve as more than just a metaphor; they are a hint to the nature of consciousness. Dreams are clues embedded in our biology, helping us understand a greater truth. In the dream, we identify with our dream character, believing that the world around us is separate from our consciousness. Then, upon waking, we come to the realization: "Oh, it was all me." While dreaming, we "forget" that our mind has crafted the entire narrative, which is why dreams feel so real. When we wake up, we don't mourn our dream avatars.

Picture a method actor who becomes so engrossed in their role that they lose sight of their true identity. Rupert Spira, a potter and teacher, has a powerful analogy with King Lear. Imagine an actor named John Smith who plays King Lear with such passion that he forgets he's not the character. He receives a standing ovation, but when a close friend visits him backstage, he finds John in distress. "Why are you sad? The audience loved your performance!" the friend asks. John laments the betrayal he experienced from his three daughters, completely lost in his role. His friend, realizing the confusion, asks, "But you're not King Lear! Who were you before you took on that role?" They trace back to a time before John was cast, and gradually, John remembers, "Oh! I was never King Lear; I've always been John Smith!"

Similarly, we must trace back the identities we cling to in order to reconnect with our true selves. We need to explore what we are beyond any identity, for identity is formed from memory. We must go beyond thought itself, as thought is merely an object; we are the subject. When we peel away identities like "I am Jai," and delve into the realm of pure thought, we can look even deeper, beyond those thoughts, to uncover what precedes everything we've ever known. Ultimately, we realize, "Ah! I was never just this human being; I have always been consciousness itself."

Imagine one is in a theater, getting ready to watch a 3D movie. On the screen are fuzzy incoherent images, but when one puts on one's 3D glasses, one suddenly seems to become immersed in the ocean. It feels like one suddenly gains a unique perspective. The blurry mix of colors and patterns on the screen represents the raw vibration of Infinite Consciousness. Putting on the 3D glasses is like when Infinite Consciousness localizes itself into finite mind, it assumes the form of perception, it puts on the activity of thinking and perceiving.

Now, one can see that one is submerged underwater, surrounded by colorful fish, vibrant coral, and lush plant life in the bright blue ocean. One can hear the gentle sounds of water, smell the salty breeze, taste the freshness of the sea, and feel the coolness enveloping oneself. One thinks to oneself, "This is incredible!" Before, there was nothing — no sights, no sounds, no textures, tastes, or scents — just patterns, vibrations, and fleeting emotions. Then Universal Consciousness punched through itself as life. Each of us is a unique viewpoint of Universal Consciousness, embodying the transcendent, the sacred, and the divine. We are Universal Mind expressing itself through different forms. Understanding this will transform one's life.

Behind the Scenes

I wanted to grasp what the world truly is, beyond its surface appearance. What was the essence of it all? The word "Maya" means illusion, suggesting that although the world is undeniably real, it isn't quite what it seems.

A vampire makes a proposition to a young man. He tells him, "After all this time, I haven't found any proof of God, just the existence of consciousness. Consciousness is the only thing in the universe that isn't an illusion, including the universe itself. The fact that you're here right now, with a choice in front of you. Live the question. I'll give you twenty-four hours to make a decision, to be or not to be a vampire." The young man ponders what it would be like to be a vampire. The weight of immortality, the insatiable thirst for blood — would he feel guilty for taking the lives of his victims just to survive? And what about transforming into a bat? What would that experience be like? There must be something incredible about soaring through the darkness using echolocation.

To be conscious means that "there is something it is like to be." It encompasses all our experiences: seeing a blue sky, hearing the ocean's roar, smelling a rose, tasting a strawberry, feeling the wind on one's skin, dreaming of a friend's face, imagining a melody, contemplating a choice, or reflecting on the experience of it all. Wow, such wonderful experiences. Consciousness remains the one thing in the universe we can be absolutely sure exists. The only certainty we have is knowing, experiencing — consciousness.

With careful and rigorous examination, computer engineer and scientist and philosopher Bernardo Kastrup presents the argument for idealism in a compelling way. I find it comforting he started his career at CERN, a mecca for some of the brightest scientists, where they built the Large Hadron Collider to study matter. It's fitting that one who was so intensely immersed in materialism and physicalism is an idealist. He's a method philosopher, one who embodies and lives out his ideas, which is always inspiring. My favorite of his books is *More Than Allegory: On religious myth, truth and belief,* a tour-de-force of scientific thought and modern myth-making. The pièce de resistance being the chapter on belief, an engaging piece of fiction writing. One poetic section is written from the perspective of a praying mantis.

Idealism is an ideal idea of the world. The physical world is wholly mental, made up of consciousness. Our inner and outer worlds are both mental. Idealism is the notion that the world is mental, but not all in one's mind. There is a world out there, separate from our individual minds but that world too is mental, made of consciousness. In idealism, the physical world is a representation. So why does the world seem physical to us? The lens of perception isn't a clear window revealing the world as it truly is. Instead, perception consists of icons — colors, sounds, scents, textures, and flavors. It does not capture the feeling of being in love, experiencing doubt, gaining profound insights, or enduring the grief of losing a loved one. These are all mental experiences.

There is only one way to truly grasp the essence of something behind just observing, and that is through one's self. When it comes to our own existence, we embody that essence. Even without a mirror or the ability to see, hear, taste, smell, or touch, we still have our inner feelings, fears, dreams, desires, imagination, and emotions. If we represent that essence, then our inner experiences are expressed in ways that others perceive as the physical presence of our body. This physical form is composed of the same atoms and forces that make up the rest of the universe, including planets, stars, and galaxies. Therefore, by understanding one's self, we can also gain insights into the world around us, like a rainbow that always seems to appear when I'm feeling genuinely happy.

When we observe the world, we can only perceive it as it appears to us; we can't grasp the world as it truly is beyond those appearances. For instance, just because she's smiling doesn't mean I fully understand her feelings; one can only see the smile on her face. The only way to truly access the essence of something is to become one with it. The inanimate objects, animals, and people we encounter are merely appearances. An appearance is incomplete, the truth of reality lies behind these appearances. Beneath the measurements we use to describe the physical world – and behind the appearances themselves – exists the thing in itself, which is fundamentally mental. It represents a movement of consciousness that presents itself to us in the form of matter.

Physicalism and materialism are hitting a physical and material brick wall. Like the Emperor in Hans Christian Andersen's *The Emperor's New Clothes*, the world may marvel at God's invisible wardrobe, but the idealist boldly proclaims, "He's not wearing any clothes!" The unifying theory is that the world is made up of *transpersonal* consciousness. Everything in the physical universe, including the moon, stars, and galaxies, is merely an appearance – how a fundamentally psychic world-soul expresses itself through our perception. All matter represents the expression of mental processes – not yours or mine, but the collective mental experiences of the universe. What's a matter, matters more than matter?

Iranian cinema is renowned for its rich storytelling, and one of its standout figures is the late great Abbas Kiarostami. His film *Close-Up* (1990) is a prime example of meta-narrative, while my personal favorite of his is *Certified Copy* (2010), along with his tribute to Japan, *Like Someone in Love* (2012), which was filmed entirely in Japan with Japanese actors. However, the Persian film that resonates with me the most is *The Mirror*, a 1997 work by Kiarostami's protégé, Jafar Panahi, who was imprisoned and banned for 20 years from writing and directing by the Iranian government.

In *The Mirror*, the camera inconspicuously follows a young girl as she rides the bus home from school. About halfway through the film, we hear a voice off-screen call out, "Cut!" This marks a striking transition as the narrative movie shifts seamlessly into a documentary film. We continue to follow the young girl, now revealed to be a child actor, as she steps off the bus and heads home. The shift is executed so boldly and nonchalantly that it's psychologically jarring; the entire world constructed by the film until that point seems to collapse, yet life proceeds as normal. Nothing changes and everything changes. By breaking the fourth wall, we gain insight into the truth behind the scenes. This film subtly illustrates that the nature of our perceived universe can be profoundly changed and it can be as simple as the cinematic trick this movie makes.

If one presses play on Pink Floyd's seminal album *The Dark Side of the Moon* at the exact moment the MGM lion roars for the third time at the beginning of the 1939 musical fantasy film *The Wizard of Oz*, and then mutes the film while turning up the music, one'll experience a synchronous symphony that's truly remarkable. Whether this alignment was intentional (think Banksy-level) or sheer coincidence, it's definitely an experience worth having. The lyrics align perfectly with the visuals, creating meaningful coincidences that enhance the viewing experience. For instance, when Glinda the Good Witch and the Wicked Witch of the West first meet, one hears, "Which is which?" and when we see the Scarecrow dancing in a field, the lyric "Lunatic on the grass" resonates beautifully. The transitions are seamless;

the songs change right at the end of scenes, such as the joyous intro of *Money* as Dorothy finally arrives in the Land of Oz.

Up until that moment, the film is in black and white, and then, in that iconic scene, she opens the door to reveal a vibrant world of Technicolor. Grasping idealism can be like living in black and white to suddenly living in a world full of color, where everything is bursting with meaning. Behind the scenes, Munchkinland holds historical significance as one of the largest gatherings of little people in the history of film. At the end of *The Wizard of Oz*, the Wizard is revealed to be just a man behind a curtain, pulling levers to maintain the illusion, while Dorothy discovers she always had the power to go home by clicking her heels three times.

One lifts the curtain to the theater of illusion to reveal God. If one takes off one's 3D glasses during a 3D movie and looks around the darkened theater, one might notice people reaching out as if they could touch the fish swimming across the screen, even though they're just illusions. These fish aren't real; they're simply representations created by the film. Consider the various objects and characters one sees in the movie — they exist only as images on the screen, not as real entities themselves. While projections are not the actual objects they depict, they do provide meaningful information about those things.

All the characters and scenes in a film draw their essence from the single screen. In the same way, everything we experience in nature — objects, animals, and people — comes from one ultimate source: Universal Consciousness. Just as the screen doesn't appear as a character in the movie yet is vital to its existence, this fundamental reality of the universe isn't visible within it, but it underlies everything we see. True reality lies beyond appearances like the screen is behind the movie. However, the screen isn't merely hidden away; it shines through as the very essence of the movie itself. Ultimately, everything in the film is essentially just the screen. In this sense, *God is the silver screen*.

For Jung, the physical world is a visible expression of the collective unconscious, which encompasses psychic and mental experiences. He perceives God as a vast mind that includes everything, with each of us being small, fragmented aspects of this greater consciousness and this essence is experiential. One can't escape experience. The divine is a unifying, universal, all-encompassing field of potential experience. The quintessence of reality is possibility.

The beauty of idealism lies in its simple elegance. Being an actor, I am a natural empath and close to my thoughts and emotions and the experiential nature of life. Maybe it's easier to access how the outside world is mental, experiential in nature too. It intuitively feels right, making sense parsimoniously. It changes how you experience the world and yourself, revealing existence in a fresh and vibrant way. It gives reality a profound significance, elevating it to something sacred. When you look up at the stars, the moon, and the Milky Way, what seems like a diverse reality is actually a single whole — its essence being consciousness.

We are immersed in the ocean of the collective unconscious, lost in oneself but this self is the world. Our personal psyches are rooted in Universal Consciousness, which is also always present in the experiential environment we inhabit as individual beings. Everything is Mind, inside Mind. We are localized perspectives of Infinite Consciousness, which perceives itself and its activities as a seemingly physical universe. In this view, the world represents the manifestation of God's thoughts. We exist within God's imagination.

When one engages with idealism as a concept, it allows one to feel things more directly. It becomes clear that other people are simply one's self in different places within the Mind, making it evident that one is seeing reflections of one's self in the lives of others. One starts to realize that the same consciousness looking out through one's eyes is inside the old lady crossing the street, the pop star performing on stage, and even a friend's cat and looking out through their eyes. It's clear that one is, in a way, the other while still being one's self. This connection is so apparent, yet it's amazing how challenging we've made it to see this truth, largely due to cultural conditioning. Films like Spike Jonze's *Being John Malkovich* and Jordan Peele's *Get Out* creatively explore this transcendent reality in fascinating ways, tapping into the deeper truths of our interconnected existence.

The yakuza boss was being released, and I had the chance to see him off. He looked so excited. "Enjoy your *katsu-don* for the both of us," I said, the go-to meal after a stint in jail. I had some good news from my lawyer, Kobayashi — an old friend had come through and secured payment for my bail, so I'd be able to leave once the thirty days were up, less than a week away. Little did I know that the toughest part of my journey was still ahead of me once I stepped out of this building. But I was mentally preparing myself for the hard road ahead, and at that moment, I was just grateful to be getting out — to see my family and friends, and have a beer.

The cherry blossom tree in the courtyard had burst into full bloom, and I suddenly thought that I might actually get to experience hanami this year after all. That winter had been especially cold, and the harsher the conditions the cherry trees face, the more vibrant and beautiful their blossoms become. Gazing out the window, a profound realization struck me — one that hasn't left my mind since. I envisioned myself as just one of the delicate sakura blossoms on this massive tree. Each of us represents a unique blossom on the immense tree of Universal Consciousness. Imagine a single cherry blossom thinking it's the center of everything. How ridiculous that would be. We all follow our own paths and rhythms, but the essence lies in taking responsibility and fulfilling our roles. The only thing we can do is to play our parts to the best of our abilities. How could this ever be solely about me? I found myself chuckling, feeling a sense of humility wash over me.

The Genuine Flower

A shift in consciousness is what some might call a spiritual awakening. A paradigm shift had occurred. This profound experience often brings with it a deep sense of mystery. Sustaining the change of worldview is challenging and of utmost importance. So, what does one do next? Make a decision amidst the chaos to stop feeling sorry for one's self. Choose to rise up once more, renewed if fortunate, and set out to make a difference in the world.

Why did ancient people make sacrifices to the gods? Fishing and rainfall for agriculture were essential for survival. Farmers often faced poor harvests due to the unpredictable forces of nature. To seek favor and balance, they offered sacrifices to Ryujin, the god who protected the ocean, as well as Mizuchi, the river god, and Zennyo Ryuo, the rain god of the mountains, all dragon deities. These sacrifices were made in the face of fear and death, hoping to transform the destructive aspects of nature into something beneficial for their lives.

Storing food ensures one won't go hungry when it gets darker and colder. Dr. Peterson's idea that sacrifice is tied to the discovery of the future is obvious and profound. Just imagine being the first person to grasp the concept of time — something we still struggle to fully understand. Consider the thought process: "I'm still hungry, but I'll save this food for later." This ability to forgo immediate pleasure for a better tomorrow is the knowledge of time passing. Without making meaningful sacrifices in the present, we can't hope to gain something better in the future. We often need to give up something we cherish to receive something good, possibly even better.

Think about the commitment involved in going to the gym regularly, eating healthily, giving up meat, fasting, or dedicating time to study and practicing a craft — all examples of choosing to sacrifice now for greater rewards later. Creating positive and productive habits takes time and discipline, but the results are worth it. Delaying gratification can lead to extraordinary rewards down the line, whether in one, five, or ten years. Can one envision a life of nightly drinking, smoking, and partying, with no exercise or studying, and still expect to be successful?

Psychological sacrifice involves letting go of unnecessary thoughts and focusing on progress. The word *susumu*, which means "to proceed," is tied to Susanoo. These ancient stories illustrate that the way out of the underworld begins with the choice to take action, which often involves making sacrifices. Instead of comparing oneself to others, the key is to look at who one was yesterday. All we can do is strive to be better than we were, moving forward.

Fantasy and drama are acting out these sacrifices. Zeami authored the influential book on dramatic theory, *Fūshikaden*, also known as *The Transmission of Style and the Flower*. It introduces the concept of the Flower, which highlights essential aspects of performance. The Flower refers to a unique grace present in an actor's portrayal — encompassing physical, psychological, and spiritual elements. It captures the audience's feeling evoked by the actor's charm and distinctiveness. The Flower symbolizes the freshness and appropriateness of exceptional acting. By completely attuning to their environment and embracing their innate nature, actors can craft appearances that are uniquely suited to each moment. This is the essence of the Flower.

Zeami discovered the essence of the Flower in the natural beauty of youth. A child's talent is akin to a flower bud that gradually blossoms, revealing its beauty. However, this bloom is temporary, and eventually, the petals will fall away. If a Noh actor mistakes the fleeting popularity that comes with being new for true acclaim, he strays from the path of the Genuine Flower. Ignoring the fleeting nature of his fame and becoming conceited is a misguided attitude. When youth brings him attention, he must remember his original purpose and work even harder. It's essential to prepare for the emergence of the Genuine Flower while the Temporary Flower is in bloom.

It is essential for a Noh actor to maintain a disciplined attitude, both for honing their craft and for performing on stage. To become the best, sacrifices are necessary, and those who practice the most discipline will earn the audience's admiration. He must recognize his shortcomings and actively work to improve. With this insight, one can plant the seed of the Genuine Flower and awaken to his true self. Zeami posited that the art of performance should be honed throughout one's lifetime. As he noted, "Natural beauty remains in an aged body," reflecting on his father's performance. Zeami often used nature as a metaphor, with my favorite being "snow in a silver bowl," symbolizing the Flower of Tranquility — a stage of life characterized by maturity and a diminished focus on ego-driven ambitions. If one can retain some beauty as one ages, then one has achieved the Genuine Flower.

Zeami consistently emphasized that even when one reaches the pinnacle of their art, it is not the ultimate objective. Humility and continual practice are vital for achieving greater mastery. A Noh actor should cherish the skills and insights gained throughout their life, whether from the innocence of childhood, the eagerness of youth while striving to become a master actor, or the fulfillment that comes from honing their abilities. From the moment an actor begins their training until they become fully seasoned, they must draw from their entire life experience and bring these narratives to life in their performances.

The life of a Noh actor is one of deep commitment and sacrifice to their craft, all for the sake of portraying a character. In a similar way, our lives involve sacrifices as we play our roles on this stage of existence. Life is sacrificial; it serves Nature in its own way. We are instruments — beautiful means to a greater purpose. Just like the cherry blossom on a sakura tree, we each have a role to fulfill in a larger story.

As Dr. Kastrup aptly expresses, "We're here in service of the divine, to the point of sacrifice." This doesn't mean we have to face death before our time; instead, it speaks to the idea that our suffering holds meaning. Through our struggles, we engage with fundamental questions about reality. Suffering brings clarity. It forces us to ask, "What is the intention of the mind?" It's only through suffering that we are prompted to confront ourselves, or else we might float through a shallow, pleasure-seeking existence. Moments of pain are often when we seek answers. "Why is the mind guiding me here?" Our suffering is not without purpose; it allows for self-reflection.

In the role of King Lear, although the actor John Smith is still present, he overlooks the understanding of his true self and must engage in self-reflection to rediscover his identity as John Smith. This mirrors the way finite mind often forgets its nature when focused on external experiences, leading them to require self-reflection to regain awareness of their true essence. John Smith needed to become King Lear to self-reflect. He needed to perform King Lear to realize he was John Smith. The finite mind has to engage in self-reflection to remember its true nature, pure consciousness. Indeed, *we are all actor*.

Susanoo's fall from the heavens can be seen as a metaphor for the dissociation of Universal Mind. When he first arrives on Earth stripped of his divine powers, Susanoo undergoes self-reflection and then puts his life on the line by facing the dragon. Similarly, when God incarnates as man in the figure of Jesus, he sacrifices his own life. By shedding his divine nature, God embraces the human experience. In essence, God dreams up the world and immerses himself in his own dream to gain self-awareness. Ultimately, life itself is a sacrificial offering to Mind of Nature. Self-reflection is our sacrifice to the divine.

purpose. Just like the cherry blossom on a sakura tree, we each have a role to fulfill in a larger story.

As Dr. Kastrup aptly expresses, "We're here in service of the divine, to the point of sacrifice." This doesn't mean we have to face death before our time. Instead, it speaks to the idea that our suffering holds meaning. Through our struggles, we engage with fundamental questions about reality. Suffering brings clarity. It forces us to ask, "What is the intention of the mind?" It's only through suffering that we are prompted to confront ourselves, or else we might float through a shallow, pleasure-seeking existence. Moments of pain are often when we seek answers: "Why is the mind guiding me here?" Our suffering is not without purpose; it allows for self-reflection.

In the role of King Lear, although the actor, John Smith, is still present, he overlooks the understanding of his true self and must engage in self-reflection to rediscover his identity as John Smith. This mirrors the way Universal Mind often forgets its nature when focused on external experiences, leading them to require self-reflection to regain awareness of their pure essence. John Smith needed to become King Lear to self-reflect. He needed to perform King Lear to realize he was John Smith. The Universal Mind has to engage in self-reflection to remember its true nature, pure consciousness. Indeed, we are all actors.

Susanoo's fall from the heavens can be seen as a metaphor for the dissociation of Universal Mind. When he first arrives on Earth, stripped of his divine powers, Susanoo undergoes self-reflection and then puts his life on the line by facing the dragon. Similarly, when God incarnates as man in the figure of Jesus, he sacrifices his own life. By shedding his divine nature, God embraces the human experience. In this way, God dreams up the world and immerses himself in his own dream to gain self-awareness. Ultimately, life itself is a sacrificial offering to Mind of Nature; self-reflection is our sacrifice to the divine.

4

Dragon of Possibility

Susanoo, who had only seen the beast from afar, approached the elderly couple to ask about the dragon called Orochi. The old man painted a vivid picture of the creature: it had eight forked heads and tails, eyes as red as winter cherries, and fir trees and cypress trees growing along its back. The dragon sprawled across eight hills and valleys as it moved.

In response, Susanoo directed the old couple and the villagers to construct eight cupboards, each filled with a tub of saké. When Orochi roared, he reassured everyone, "Don't run! No more children will be taken today! Quickly fill eight vats with saké and bring them to the town square!" The villagers, trusting Susanoo, eagerly complied.

As Susanoo sat perched on a rooftop, he caught sight of the dragon approaching, its eight heads snarling and eyes glowing red. One head spotted a vat of saké, and soon the others were drawn in as well, all eager for the drink. The dragon's heads quickly drank from the vats, and before long, Orochi succumbed to drunkenness. Seizing the moment, Susanoo rallied the villagers to attack and swiftly beheaded the dragon with his sword.

Possibility of Dragon

Dragon veins, also known as dragon lines, are a concept from *feng shui*, which literally translates to "wind-water." This ancient Chinese practice focuses on using energy forces to harmonize individuals with their environments. In this context, dragon veins refer to channels of energy that flow through mountain ranges, representing underground pathways of Qi. Various landscapes and bodies of water were believed to influence the direction of these cosmic currents of universal Qi.

I've been living in Shibuya, a unique ward of Tokyo, for twenty-five years. The name Shibuya literally means "harsh valley," and its kanji pictographically represents "where water accumulates from four directions." For over a decade, I've called Kamiyamachō home, a peaceful neighborhood that translates to "God Mountain Town." Located in the quieter part of Shibuya, known as Oku-shibu, it's known for its trendy restaurants and bars, and lies along a ley line that connects Mount Fuji, Meiji Shrine, and the Imperial Palace, making it one of the strongest "power spots" in the Tokyo metropolitan area.

For the past twelve years, my house has been nestled between the expansive headquarters of the Church of Perfect Liberty and the Japanese headquarters for the Unification Church, also known as the Family Federation for World Peace and Unification. The Unification Church, founded by South Korean leader Sun Myung Moon — who claimed to be the Messiah and the Second Coming of Christ — has many followers worldwide colloquially called "Moonies." The religious cult is famous for its Blessing ceremonies, stadium-filled mass weddings where thousands of brides and grooms are married by the leader at the same time.

Former Prime Minister Shinzo Abe lived just a two-minute walk away from me, and when he was tragically assassinated in 2022, the very next day, I visited his home to pay my respects, witnessing the arrival of his body to his grieving widow. Abe's death was a shocking act carried out by a man who blamed him for his family's bankruptcy due to the Unification Church. It struck me as strange how intertwined the two entities were, both in terms of fate and physical proximity. Just a year prior, in 2021, Donald Trump and Shinzo Abe both spoke at the Rally of Hope, an event organized by the Unification Church.

The real reason I call Shibuya home is Yoyogi Kōen, Tokyo's version of Central Park. I'm an avid runner and I used to own a dog so I wanted to be close to the park and take him on walks. It's a refreshing oasis of greenery right in the middle of the city's chaos. With the powerful Meiji Jingū shrine adjacent to the park, there's a mysterious spiritual energy and atmosphere to Yoyogi Kōen that parks I've been to in Europe and North America don't seem to have.

The park played a significant role during the post-World War II era when the General Headquarters (GHQ) of the Allied Powers was established in Japan. After Japan's surrender in 1945, General Douglas MacArthur led the GHQ from Tokyo, and the area that is now Yoyogi Park once housed US military personnel in a community called Washington Heights. It was a little world for ex-pats, complete with its own post office and movie theater. I can only imagine the feeling of that time, shaped by the aftermath of war. As Japan began to rebuild, the military housing was gradually taken down, and the land was repurposed to serve as the athletes' village for the 1964 Tokyo Olympics. In 1967, Yoyogi Park was officially opened, transforming it into a spacious public park and cultural hub in the heart of Tokyo. Its rich history, marked by its connection to the post-war period and its evolution into a community space, reminds us of Japan's resilience and its dedication to creating inviting green spaces for everyone to enjoy.

In the summer, the heat and humidity make it too uncomfortable to run during the day, so I prefer to go at dusk when it cools down a bit. The park features a distinct landscape design, and I usually run along the 2.7 km outer trail. Interestingly, this trail was used by the Ethiopian long-distance runners as a warm-up during the 1964 Olympics. They praised the soft dirt path, dotted with branches and leaves, for being easy on the knees and helping to strengthen ankle muscles. One time, after completing two laps around the park, I realized to my dismay that there was a hole in my secret change pocket, and my 100 yen and 50 yen coins were gone. It was getting dark, so I switched on my phone's flashlight and retraced my steps through the thicker part of the forest trail near Meiji Jingū. Finding my coins meant I could buy a drink and run another lap.

This section of the park sometimes gives me an eerie feeling; there were stories about the grounds being the site of mass suicides during the war—where soldiers preferred death over defeat. The earlier rain made the ground damp and soft, and as I walked back, I spotted something shiny near a tree. My 100 yen coin! I couldn't find the other 50 yen coin, so I consoled myself by saying that this was a toll I needed to pay to the gods for allowing me to run in the park. As I bent down to pick up the coin, I caught movement out of the corner of my eye. What I saw took my breath away. There, in the middle of a pile of dead wet leaves, were a pair of snakes, twisting and writhing. As I got closer, I realized it was two snakes mating, winding around each other in an erotic frenzy. I drew even closer, shining my phone light, their scales mostly rich brown, with hints of red and orange as they coiled around each other in an infinity loop. It was grotesque, yet mesmerizing. Just as I was absorbed in the spectacle, I shifted the light a little to my right and felt my heart race. There, watching me, were two giant brown toads, each larger than my fist, side by side. I screamed.

In Japanese, the word — *kemonomichi* — which translates to "trail of beasts," refers to a dark, uncertain path in the forest that we metaphorically sometimes find ourselves on, where the unknown sparks our imagination and survival instincts. Startled, I jumped back, watching the toads exchange glances with their calm, wise eyes just before I sprinted away in fear, crashing straight into a massive spider's web. Being deep in the dark is like being trapped inside a cave or an insect hive, filling one with an unnerving awareness that something is behind one's self, even if one can't see it. It's that horror movie moment when one knows not to turn around, but feels compelled to do so. It's instinctual — a reminder of our evolution, where our senses have adapted for survival, making us anticipate the worst. Potential danger lurks in the unknown. Potential is predatory.

When a character in a story makes an error, falls off the pathway, deviates from what they know they should do, it produces a state of internal chaos, they don't know what to do. This is often symbolized by an encounter with a monster, like a dragon or something under the water, like a sea monster that swallows you and pulls you down. Pinocchio swallowed by the leviathan, Moby Dick, Jonah and the whale. Like you are walking on thin ice and there's a shark swimming underneath it. Peter Pan and the crocodile, Steve Spielberg's *Jaws*. Why? We've been prey animals for a very long time. How many times has an ancestor of ours been at a watering hole and then attacked by an alligator and eaten? Our ancestors have been in a battle with carnivorous reptiles for millennia. The fear and fascination we have for dinosaurs is undeniable, again, Spielberg's *Jurassic Park*; he knows what scares us. Even when dinosaurs roamed the earth, we had a common mammalian ancestor, we were once rodents. It's worth noting that the word for dinosaur in Japanese is *kyōryū*, a combination of the kanjis for "fear" and "dragon."

I spent some time on the island of Komodo in Indonesia location hunting for a shampoo ad starring Japanese fashion icon Akimoto Kozue, daughter of my favorite sumo wrestler, *yokozuna* Chiyonofuji Mitsugu, nicknamed The Wolf. We ended up shooting in the Philippines but that's besides the point. I assure everyone there is nothing more visceral than being chased by a gigantic lizard that eats whole water buffaloes. The Komodo Dragons have venom in their saliva for crissakes. The Komodo Dragon evokes primordial fear. Do you know what animal kills the most humans every year? Besides the bloody mosquito, it is the snake. Show a snake to some monkeys for the first time, they will immediately jump to safety and stare at it all day. They're mesmerized but scared. We are fascinated with snakes. When we see one, we freeze, like when encountering the basilisk in *Harry Potter and the Chamber of Secrets* or Medusa in Greek mythology, we turn to stone.

During the Covid-19 state of emergency, Yoyogi Kōen was cordoned off for three months, and no one was allowed in. When the park finally reopened, my girlfriend and I were among the first to return, excited to revive our daily walks. However, as soon as we stepped into the park, she was suddenly struck on the back of her head. A crow had attacked her and swooped past us, cawing as if to say, "This is our territory!" To our surprise, we discovered she had scratches on her scalp, the marks left by the crow's claws. She said the impact was so strong that she initially thought a person had hit her. Since that incident, she has developed a fear of crows — a case of what we call "corvid trauma." If one takes a close look at a crow's feet, one can see how fierce they are. I've been told that my own crow's feet are charming. A murder of crows began to circle above; it seemed that after being away for so long, the crows had taken over the park.

As we continued our walk, we spotted a sign near some unique Japanese Pagoda Trees that we must have walked by a hundred times before, yet we had never noticed. The sign read "Dragon's Claw Tree" (*Sophora japonica*), explaining that the branches resembled dragon claws. If you look closely at a dragon's claws, they are quite similar to a bird of prey's talons. When I shot the film *My Little Guidebook: Ice* in Hokkaido, I played an experimental nature photographer named Luke who has a spiritual relationship with a fox. We filmed the formidable Steller's Sea Eagle up close. The powerful raptor has an over two-meter wingspan, and its large yellow talons with sharp black claws are exactly like a dragon's. In fact, a dragon, just like an eagle, has both talons and wings. As we continued our walk in the park, we passed a stone sculpture that we also had overlooked many times before, and upon closer inspection, we saw it was a statue of Quetzalcoatl, the feathered serpent god from Aztec mythology. We didn't expect to find a Mexican dragon in Yoyogi Park.

The dragon can be thought of as a snake with talons and wings. In Greek mythology, earth and sky — represented by Gaia and Uranus — combine to create everything in between. The grounded snake represents earth and substance, while the flying bird represents the sky and psyche. The winged reptile symbolizes the union of matter and spirit. In Norse mythology, the journey of the soul is depicted as a descent represented by the serpent, leading into the depths of darkness and the mythological underworld — a place of struggle and pain. At the bottom, we can discover our gift and the light, which allows us to embark on the spirit's journey, represented by an eagle's ascent. This complete journey — combining the serpent's descent and the eagle's rise — is symbolized by the dragon. By traversing both paths, one can transcend.

Most of us are familiar with the iconic image of three wise Japanese macaques covering their eyes, ears, and mouth, symbolizing "see no evil, hear no evil, speak no evil." For the sake of this discussion, let's tweak the three mystical apes' maxim to: "see evil in the sky, hear evil in the tree, speak evil in the grass." Interestingly, monkeys have three distinct calls for different threats: one for danger from above, like predatory birds; another for threats in the trees, such as big cats; and a third for dangers lurking in the grass, like snakes. These are the creatures that can pose a real risk if one isn't careful. Could the dragon be a fusion of these predatory animals, created by our imagination as a response to millions of years of being hunted by fearsome beings in the darkness?

In his book *An Instinct for Dragons*, anthropologist David E. Jones says there are dragons in every culture including the Inuit who have never seen a reptile. If there were ever evidence for the existence of the collective unconscious, dragons would be it. The image of the dragon represents an amalgam of the principal predators of ancestral humans: raptors, leopards and pythons. A chimera, after all, is a creature made up of parts from various animals. It represents what we envision when we encounter the unknown, especially in moments of fear — much like a child's imagination conjuring monsters hiding under the bed. The concept of an abstract predator embodies those lurking threats in the shadows. I have a fascination with chimeras. Consider the Kirin, a dragon that resembles a deer, often likened to an Asian unicorn, which ranks as the third most powerful mythical creature, following only the dragon and the phoenix. Then there's the Griffin from Roman mythology, a majestic being that is half lion and half eagle, alongside the Sphinx from Egypt, a combination of lion, eagle, and woman. Even *Pokémon*, "pocket monsters," can be considered chimeras.

Interestingly, the legendary Japanese *kaijū*, Gojira, known as "Godzilla" in the West, which seems to blend the words "God" with "lizard," actually wasn't originally conceived as a reptilian creature. I once shared with Nicolas Cage, an avid Gojira fan, the origin of Gojira's name, which is a portmanteau of the Japanese words *gorira* (gorilla) and *kujira* (whale). He was genuinely surprised and said, "I didn't know that." Gojira's design draws inspiration from the gorilla, and her aquatic abilities come from her whale heritage. Nick recognized the term "kujira" because his favorite Japanese whiskey is named Kujira, an Okinawan whiskey that's quite rare, which he stocks up on during his trips to Japan. It's curious how radioactivity spawns heroes like Superman and Spiderman in America, while it creates monsters in Japan. The film *Gojira* (1954) emerged from the aftermath of nuclear warfare, and the memories of Hiroshima and Nagasaki continue to loom large in the collective consciousness of Japan and the world.

Dragon Striking Down Lion by Leonardo da Vinci, 1515

Little dragon. The renowned zoologist Masanori Hata, better known by his nickname "Mutsugoro," played my father in a short film titled *Bus Panic!!*, featuring the iconic boy band SMAP. When the film was submitted to international festivals and required English subtitles, the writer worried that audiences outside Japan might not recognize who Mutsugoro was. As a result, they opted for the subtitle "Animalfucker" upon his reveal. His controversial reputation often preceded him; he was rumored to have engaged in a long-term relationship with his pet bear, a situation categorized as zoophilia.

Over lunch I eagerly jumped at the chance to ask Mutsugoro, notorious for his perilous encounters with wildlife, about the scariest animal he had ever encountered. He recounted his experience in Africa, where a parasitic worm had burrowed a hole through the bottom of his foot. Initially, he hadn't noticed it because of its small size. This parasite feeds off its host's nutrients, growing larger and slowly migrating upwards, potentially reaching the brain and resulting in death if left untreated.

To remove the worm, he had to locate it and pierce his skin on his upper leg, then carefully wind it out with a small rod. He explained that it needed to be extracted slowly, for if one pulled too hard, it could break off inside his body and disappear. The Rod of Asclepius, the symbol of medicine we still use today, is reminiscent of this process. He described the pain as excruciating, which I found to be the most terrifying story I had ever heard. When I got home, I researched it and discovered it was the Guinea worm, scientifically known as *dracunculus*, which translates to "little dragon" in Latin.

Sea Kingdom of the Dragon God

The most influential Japanese fairy tale is the story of *Urashima Tarō*. Once upon a time there lived a young man called Urashima. One day he rescued a turtle which had been caught by children. A few days later the turtle took Urashima to the Dragon Palace at the bottom of the sea in order to repay his kindness. Urashima was moved by the beauty of the palace. The princess Oto-hime welcomed him with her beautiful maids. Urashima was very happy to stay there for three days. When he wished to return the princess gave him a jeweled casket saying that he should not open it under any circumstances. When he returned home, he was astonished to find 300 years had passed since he had left. Completely desperate, he opened the casket in spite of the princess' warning, whereupon white smoke came out of the box and Urashima turned into an old man.

The box of smoke left a strong impression, a cautionary tale that if one lives a life of hedonism, it'll come back to bite one's self. Hardly anyone born in Japan does not know this story. *Urashima Tarō* was a formidable fairy tale in my life. The archetype of Eternal Youth brings to mind the phenomenon known as Peter Pan syndrome and carries deep significance in understanding the Japanese psyche. This archetype is influential, and just being aware of its existence can help from being taken over by the powerful narrative pattern.

This character is perpetually caught in a state of "not yet," unable to fully grasp reality or find the genuine experiences of life. The Eternal Youth struggles to conform to societal norms, convinced that surrendering his unique talents would be a tremendous loss. He defends his viewpoint by arguing that adapting to societal expectations is unnecessary, dismissing the world as flawed for not recognizing his exceptional gifts. Then one day we witness this youthful spirit attempting a sudden ascent, eager to display his extraordinary artistry or to take on the role of the world's savior. His moment of brilliance and powerful presence may captivate those around him, but unfortunately, he often lacks the durability and tenacity needed to sustain this success — a common weakness of this archetype.

In these brief flashes of courage, he is seen as a brave soul, yet beneath this bravado lies a yearning to return to the comforting embrace of the Great Mother. This deep longing may lead him to flirt with self-destruction, sometimes even courting death as a manifestation of his desire. If he is wise enough to evade death, he may find himself in a period of aimlessness, navigating life without purpose. Yet, eventually, he will make another attempt to ascend in an entirely new way. He engages in dazzling pursuits, chasing after the fleeting interests of the moment but often without consistency. This is the pattern of Eternal Youth.

Urashima Tarō shares a deep bond with his mother, a relationship that profoundly influences his life. At the age of 40 (in some versions), he still lives in her home and goes on solitary fishing trips, returning each time empty-handed and feeling isolated amidst the vast ocean. This scenario vividly illustrates a sense of regression. In this state, the ego often uncovers valuable insights through its connection to the unconscious. While there may be elements of pathology or negativity associated with regression, it can also be the source of new growth and potential. Fairy tales that reflect our psychological development often start with themes of regression, laying the groundwork for transformation. For regression to be creative, something new must emerge, and the ego needs to strive to integrate that new element.

The new element that enters our hero's life is a beautiful woman. Tarō's perception of time shifts the moment he steps into the unconscious realm and meets her. To break the strong bond with his mother, he needs to encounter a woman who embodies a different kind of attraction than she does. Once every century, the enchanting Oto-hime, princess of the underwater palace Ryūgū-jō, transforms into a turtle and visits Sumiyoshi Shrine to pray. On this occasion, she gets caught by some children, but Urashima Tarō comes to her rescue. Later, at the Dragon Palace under the sea, he meets the turtle princess again, where she proposes to him. Lacking knowledge about her true identity, Urashima is captivated and follows her. In this tale, rather than winning a woman through a heroic battle, our hero finds himself ensnared by her charm.

Urashima Tarō, enchanted by the turtle princess, marries her and spends many years apart from the world above. However, he eventually returns home (in some versions without marrying her) and faces a sudden and tragic fate, rapidly aging into an old man. This transformation might be a natural consequence for a youth drawn to a woman reminiscent of his mother. Japanese Jungian psychologist Hayao Kawai, a senior professor at Kyoto University, explains how the Japanese feminine figure characteristically is divided in two. One is a turtle princess living under the sea who strongly emphasizes the physical aspect; the other is the princess who refuses all proposals and ascends to heaven. She lives in the heavenly realm as an Eternal Girl who would not be a marriage partner. The Eternal Girl would be a perfect match for a Japanese Eternal Youth.

Urashima Tarō was too unprepared, marrying Princess Oto as she seduced him, then getting homesick and coming back, all without much thought. Therefore, it is extremely significant that it was at such a time that the princess gave him a jeweled casket. "If you could not forget me and would like to visit me again, please never open the casket." This was the last chance for Urashima's willpower. To deal with the emergence of a new element, when regression is creative, a hero has to involve himself, take action with vigor and energy. Urashima made too little effort, a familiar pattern. Could this archetype be playing out prevalently right now in the broader culture of Japan? The theme of "forbidden" relating to the jeweled casket resembles that of "Don't look" from *The Crane Wife*. Urashima was too weak. That's why suddenly becoming an old man seems unavoidable.

There is an idealism version of the ending. Urashima opens the jeweled casket fully aware that it contains 8000 years of life. He still opens it knowing he'll instantly grow old in order to show that he himself is Urashima Tarō. In this version there are three jeweled boxes. One has the feather of a crane, the second box is the puff of smoke that makes him old, and the third box contains a mirror. Self-reflection. This "Willed Urashima" is a way of overcoming the image of Urashima Tarō as an eternal youth.

The Dragon Palace, a recurring theme in Japanese fairy tales, beautifully captures the complexity of the Japanese psyche. For many in Japan, the sea symbolizes an eternal maternal presence. Descriptions of the Dragon Palace reveal spring in the east window, summer in the south, autumn in the west, and winter in the northern window, illustrating how the palace exists outside the constraints of time. Characters like Urashima Tarō highlight the idea of timelessness in the unconscious. He remains eternally young, lost in an unconscious realm where he simply forgets that time is passing.

Returning to everyday life after experiencing a different world can be incredibly challenging. In Jungian psychology, this "other world" refers to the unconscious. One notable aspect of Japanese culture is the lack of a clear distinction between the external and internal worlds, as well as between the conscious and unconscious. For the Japanese, the barrier separating this world from the next is surprisingly thin, resembling the delicate nature of *fusuma* (sliding room dividers) and *shoji* (paper screen doors). This reflects the essence of the Japanese ego. By keeping boundaries fluid, Japanese consciousness seeks to perceive existence as an undifferentiated whole. This fluidity helps explain why Japanese fairy tales often feel more akin to myths and legends.

The legend of *Urashima Tarō* has in the course of time become a fairy tale that modern Japanese know well. There's something about this story that resonates deeply with the Japanese psyche. As James Hillman noted during one of his visits to Japan, "The Japanese prefer aesthetic solutions to conflicts." Hayao, a former Minister of Culture, elaborates on this idea in *The Japanese Psyche*. He points out that when Westerners hear the term "Dragon Palace," they often think of a battle with a dragon, while for the Japanese, it brings to mind the palace's inherent beauty. Hayao explains that the rich descriptions of nature found in Japanese fairy tales serve a purpose similar to the dragon battles in Western stories.

In Western narratives, the hero often slays the dragon and then marries, symbolizing the reconciliation of opposing forces. On the other hand, the aesthetic harmony portrayed through the Four Seasons in Japanese culture embodies the same theme of unity without conflict. Urashima Tarō doesn't engage in a dragon fight; instead, the story concludes with a sense of melancholy. For the Japanese, a scene of natural beauty is often viewed as more fulfilling than a conventional happy ending.

FEAR

Face Everything And Rise

I have fond memories of my time in London with my actor friend Hiroyuki Ikeuchi when we were 24 in 2001. We would often listen to Ian Brown's song *F.E.A.R.*, where every lyric is an acronym for "fear." The music video was pretty dope too; it played in reverse. Whenever you read a FEAR, sing it just like Ian Brown.

For Each a Road

To tell stories we needed to personify chaos. Picture this: a dragon rising up from the depths of the unknown. In the oldest Babylonian myth, chaos is depicted as a female dragon. This Eternal Dragon of Chaos is a constant threat to the safety of the city. It can take on many forms — terrifying creatures, deceitful people, and even the darker aspects of ourselves. However, those who stay alert and hold fast to their ethical principles can see this threat clearly and choose to stand up against it.

False Evidence Appearing Real

The Orochi is a dragon with eight heads and eight tails, similar to the nine-headed Hydra from Greek mythology — cut off one head, and three more grow back. But what does this multi-headed dragon symbolize? When one ignores paying taxes or bills, they pile up and pull one deeper into trouble and debt. Overlooking a problem only makes the dragon grow bigger and harder to face. The Great Red Dragon in Revelations has seven heads, much like the seven-headed Naga I encountered during my time in Cambodia. So how does one respond when one is confronted by a multi-headed dragon?

Fuck Everything and Run

Running away isn't the answer; one can't escape one's destiny. When hope seems lost, what should one do? Just give up?

No, it's important to change one's perspective. Things start to fall apart when one ignores reality, so one needs to open one's eyes and truly see what's around one's self. The word "Draco" in Latin and "Drakon" in Greek both mean "serpent" or "dragon." The roots of these words suggest "to watch" or "to guard closely," originating from the Greek term "drakōn," which means "gazing." If we fail to keep our eyes open in the depths of the underworld, we may face greater suffering, and the consequences could be dire.

Fatal Ends and Resurrections

What should we do when the unexpected happens in our lives? We have to grow to become brave enough to face the dragon. By simply standing one's ground with a tough kind of love. Here I am, ready to engage, without giving ground, without giving way. When chaos takes over, the first step is to face what we may prefer to avoid. Tackling those challenges is essential for navigating through the turmoil and restoring order.

Fateful Endings and Regret

One might have experienced betrayal, a serious illness, job loss, or even a natural disaster. Perhaps one knows one needs to take action, but fear keeps one from doing so, causing one to procrastinate. If one lets it go on for too long, one may find oneself feeling completely overwhelmed and sinking deeper into chaos. Don't shy away from one's destiny — whatever it may be. It's happening to me, because only I can overcome it. *Amor Fati.* Embrace one's fate.

Forever Evolve and Regress

The capacity to respond to malevolence, or "response ability," raises difficult questions about moral choices in extreme circumstances. For instance, if one were born and raised in 1920s Germany and became a Nazi soldier, would one truly have acted differently? The gas chambers built to execute millions of Jews were designed to be more humane for the perpetrators, a disturbing notion, to ease the stress of mass killing as the Nazis believed they were doing good. The war crimes committed by Unit 731 exemplify humanity's potential for unimaginable cruelty, influenced by cultural, historical, and personal factors. Our susceptibility to external influences reminds us that the horrors like the Third Reich are not a distant memory.

Face Evil and Respond

Who does one encounter first when they fall into chaos? Godzilla of Chaos, one's self. We must remain vigilant not only about others' actions but also our own inner dragon, acknowledging our own capacity for evil. Bitterness and resentment can lead one closer to that darkness. The ultimate dragon lies within. Psychologically, one must have a relationship with their dragon and not become infused with it. It's vital to stay aware and attentive, and be in conversation with our dragon. Merely claiming one would never do wrong isn't enough; recognizing one's potential for evil is essential to prevent it. Understanding this darker side is necessary for transformation.

For Every Action, Responsibility

Ultimately, to face evil one must become the dragon. Standing up for good and saying, "It's not okay," is the requirement of becoming a dragon. In the arts, the art that moved people came from artists who alchemized the fallout of evil acts, for better or for worse. By integrating one's Shadow, one can channel negative energy into creativity.

For Everyone a Religion

Don't be too certain about the uncertain. We all seek meaning and strive to be heroic against evil forces. Acknowledging our own capacity for evil makes us less vulnerable to false narratives and misinformation, which oversimplify the world by clearly labeling "bad guys" and offering easy answers to chaos. Life is complex, and there are no simple solutions. Understanding that we contain both angels and demons helps us avoid blaming others and encourages personal responsibility.

Fake Emotions Affect Reality

We always live within a story, a myth, even the idea of living without one is a myth. Recognizing our susceptibility to narrative patterns is a good starting point. Being aware of the good and evil within us fosters introspection and ultimately makes us wiser as we reflect on ourselves.

Forget Everything and Remember

Remember one's roots. In *The Lion King*, when Simba is engulfed in despair, he is guided by the mandrill shaman Rafiki and sees his father's face reflected in the waters of the lake. Mufasa materializes in the sky as a storm cloud, instructing him, "You have forgotten who you are, and so forgotten me. Look inside yourself, Simba; you are more than what you have become. Remember who you are." In our darkest moments, connecting with our ancestors can be a source of strength. By confronting the unknown, we can rise above suffering and fulfill our true potential.

For Everything a Reason

Everything one does, every action one takes is meaningful.

The Dragon Chef

The Chinese dragon has a rich history, and I find it visually a bit more akin to a liger (half lion, half tiger) than its more serpentine Japanese counterpart. Some people say that the Chinese dragon, which typically has four or five claws depending on whether it's an ordinary or an Imperial symbol, lost a few claws on its journey to Japan, where the Japanese dragon has only three claws.

There's a good Chinese hot pot, or *hinabe,* restaurant in the Shinsen district of Shibuya called Lao Maa, which is open until 3 a.m. and is beautifully decorated with Chinese red lanterns (origin of the red-light district) and stunning images of Chinese dragons. I have a regular table with a perfect view of the projection screen that plays Jackie Chan movies on a loop. The wall behind the screen is plastered with posters of his films, including *Dragon Fist, Dragon Lord, Heart of Dragon, Rising Dragon, Twin Dragons, Dragon Heat,* and *Dragon Blade.* My girlfriend always orders a Dragon highball, a concoction with Shaoxing wine. One standout dish is the *yodaredori,* a broiled chicken breast dish served with a delicious *mala* sauce, a seasoning made from Sichuan peppercorns and red chilies. Mala combines two Chinese characters that mean "numbing" and "spicy," reflecting the tingling sensation from the Sichuan pepper and the heat of the red chili.

Just as Chinese and Japanese dragons share similarities, the Chinese Sichuan peppercorn and Japanese peppercorn, known as *sanshō,* are also related. Sanshō has a slightly lemony flavor and provides a unique tingly numbness, making it wonderful for seasoning various Japanese dishes, particularly grilled eel, *unagi.* It's as ubiquitous at Japanese restaurants as salt and pepper are in the West, often found alongside *shichimi,* a seven-spice *tōgarashi* (red chili) blend that sometimes includes *yuzu* peel. This yuzu shichimi is perfect for sprinkling on tempura, soba, and udon for an extra burst of flavor. Yuzu, a tart Japanese citrus fruit, is also combined with green chili to create a special seasoning called *yuzu koshō,* or yuzu pepper, which pairs wonderfully with *nabemono* and *yakitori.* My love for chili peppers runs deep — I even played Tōgarashi-Man in a Nissin Cup Noodles commercial.

You are what you eat. *Ryōri no Tetsujin*, or *Iron Chef*, is a Japanese cooking competition show that first aired on Fuji TV in the late 1990s, paving the way for reality television. The format pits a challenger chef against one of the established "Iron Chefs," who are renowned culinary experts. Initially, there were four Iron Chefs: Iron Chef Japanese, Iron Chef Chinese, Iron Chef French, and Iron Chef Italian. Each episode features a secret ingredient, and the chefs have one hour to create multiple dishes highlighting that ingredient. A panel of experts then judges their creations to determine the winner.

The show was hosted by the charismatic Takeshi Kaga, a well-known Japanese actor, who portrayed the flamboyant Chairman Kaga. The Chairman brought his unique vision to life by designing a stunning cooking arena known as Kitchen Stadium. Here, chefs from around the world competed against his team of Iron Chefs. Always dressed in eye-catching formal attire, Chairman Kaga would kick off each episode with his signature opening line, "Si je me souviens bien…" inspired by Arthur Rimbaud, followed by the memorable command, "Allez Cuisine!" The show gained immense popularity globally and has inspired numerous spin-offs and adaptations in different countries. I am honored and thrilled to be part of this legacy as the grand-nephew of Kaga-san, serving as the Chairman of *Iron Chef Canada*. I never would have imagined I would have the opportunity to take on this role.

In Japanese, the word for "delicious" is *umai*. Japanese cuisine is celebrated worldwide for its careful preparation and beautiful presentation. When food is arranged on a plate, it resembles a carefully composed painting, sometimes with a message like evoking the essence of autumn. The Japanese culture cherishes the unique qualities of each ingredient, valuing the importance of their individual flavors and textures. Historically, the early Japanese diet was quite simple, consisting of fish, vegetables, fruits, and seaweed.

In the early 19th century, Kikunae Ikeda, a Japanese scientist and professor at Tokyo Imperial University, tasted the *dashi* soup stock that his wife made for their boiled tofu. He couldn't help but wonder what made it taste so exceptional. When he asked her, she replied that it was the *konbu* – the dried kelp she used to make it. Strangely, this flavor reminded him of the taste of certain foods from his time studying in Germany. Curious about why konbu imparted such a unique flavor to the soup, he dedicated himself to discovering the substance responsible for his wife's irresistibly umai dashi. Japanese soups are traditionally made using dashi, a simple and clear broth. This stock is created by extracting flavors from brown algae known as konbu (Saccharina japonica) and from *katsuobushi*, which are flakes of bonito fish that have been cooked, salted, dried, fermented, and smoked. Dashi is rich in umami and is a foundational component of Japanese cuisine, essential to many dishes.

Have you ever spent a summer day in a garden, picked a ripe, juicy tomato and taken a bite? The experience is pure umami. Umami is recognized as the fifth taste, alongside the traditional four: sweetness, saltiness, sourness, and bitterness. Together, these tastes shape our overall perception of flavor. While spiciness adds a kick, it's more of an accent rather than a basic taste on its own. If one pays close attention, one'll notice a common thread running through the complex flavors of foods like asparagus, tomatoes, cheese, and meat. There's something special, a nuance that stands apart from the four main tastes and deserves recognition as a primary quality since it can't be replicated by mixing the others. This taste can be quite subtle and often gets overshadowed by bolder flavors, making it hard to identify unless one really focuses on it.

Professor Ikeda noticed that the taste of his wife's konbu dashi was distinct from sweet, sour, bitter, or salty. By 1908, he isolated crystals that captured this unique flavor. These crystals were composed of glutamate, a common amino acid found in many foods and in our bodies. A year later, he figured out how to mass-produce this substance, partly by combining glutamate with sodium, which not only made it flavorful but also easy to use as a seasoning and digest. He invented monosodium glutamate, or MSG. However, he faced one challenge: how to describe this taste. It was savory — almost meaty — but derived from konbu. So, he gave it a temporary name until he could think of something better. He called it "umami." Through his work, Professor Ikeda identified, named, and synthesized this fundamental taste, mass-producing it as Ajinomoto, which means "Essence of Flavor" — essentially umami in a bottle. Today, Ajinomoto stands as one of the world's largest multinational industrial companies and is one of the jewels of Japanese industry.

Ikeda remarked, "If our only experiences with sweetness were limited to carrots or milk, our understanding of what 'sweet' truly means would be as vague as our grasp of umami's distinctive flavor. Just as honey and sugar give us a clear sense of sweetness, the salts found in glutamic acid could provide a similarly clear understanding of this unique taste." He insightfully pointed out that the connection between salt and glutamate could transform the way soy sauce is made, as it embodies both salty and umami flavors. This unique flavor combination might also shed light on the popularity of ketchup in Western cuisine. Following Ikeda's discovery, the use of MSG in food became an overnight sensation in Japan and China. In the West, it gained particular traction within the burgeoning Chinese restaurant sector, especially in the United States.

One unforgettable childhood taste memory I have is of a Japanese candy called Miyako Konbu — a thinly sliced piece of pickled konbu coated in a white "magic powder," about the size of a stick of gum. The combination of sour and umami on my taste buds completely amazed my young North American palate. What's fascinating about umami is that when glutamate interacts with other flavors, particularly another umami source, there's a synergistic effect that significantly boosts the overall flavor intensity. The resulting taste is more potent than one would expect by simply adding the individual flavors together.

Ikeda had stumbled upon the secret behind the magical properties of dashi, the combination of konbu and katsuobushi, the textbook example of umami synergy. Even small amounts of one ingredient can greatly enhance the flavor of another. This also helps explain why vegetarian broth made with konbu and shiitake mushrooms delivers such a robust umami flavor. Tomatoes and tuna — what a delightful umami pairing! It's interesting to note that most languages don't have a single term for this taste sensation. Unlike Japanese cuisine, which has dashi as a universally acknowledged ingredient for adding umami, Western cuisines lack a widely recognized counterpart. In Japan, dashi is intrinsically linked with the fifth taste and acts as a vital source of savoriness in a cuisine that uses minimal fat.

In every *Iron Chef Canada* battle, I introduce my Culinary Curveball — an unexpected ingredient that the chefs must integrate into one of their dishes. In Battle Pork, that surprise ingredient was cheese curds, a key element of the beloved French-Canadian comfort food, poutine. "My dash(i) is sick," said the charming young chef from Montreal, whose remarkable cooking had truly impressed me. Hearing him say that filled me with pride. With the rising popularity of sushi and Japanese cuisine, terms like *dashi, mirin, yuzu, saké, tōgarashi, ume, shiso,* and other words have become familiar to chefs and food enthusiasts worldwide, highlighting the significant influence of Japanese culinary traditions. Danny "Smiles" Francis, aptly known as Chef Smiles, is a blend of Egyptian and Italian heritage, and he owns the Montreal restaurant le Violon, which now occupies the space once filled by Maison Publique.

As the Chairman of *Iron Chef Canada*, one of my favorite dishes from that incredible show was Chef Smiles' baba ghanoush with pork belly shawarma. His father hails from Alexandria, Egypt, making this dish a tribute to his roots. The grilled pork was prepared in a shawarma style, expertly seasoned with spices. The deep flavor and rich color of the baba ghanoush were extraordinary; I had never seen eggplant turn such a striking dark gray. The smoky baba ghanoush paired perfectly with the charred pork. A sprinkle of roasted pine nuts and vibrant pomegranate seeds added a delightful nutty and tart contrast, making it truly sublime. His upset victory in Battle Pork against Iron Chef Susur Lee was well-earned but I knew Iron Chef Lee would come back strong in the next battle.

Susur Lee, a celebrated Hong Kong-born Canadian chef and Iron Chef, is renowned for his quick knife cutting skills and charisma. With restaurants in Singapore, Washington DC, and New York, he was also a co-owner of a Toronto restaurant with Drake. Lee's Asian fusion style combines Eastern flavors with European techniques, earning him a spot as one of the "10 Hottest Chefs" by *Food and Wine* magazine. He is a devoted family man and embodies class, with a strong affinity for seafood as he grew up surrounded by the ocean in Hong Kong.

Susur Lee's second *Iron Chef Canada* duel was against challenger Paul Boehmer, in Battle Tiny Fish. Both chefs showcased their culinary talents through various inventive dishes involving tiny fish, with the first round ending with the challenger leading 12–10. Iron Chef Lee's offerings included a sautéed shrimp dish with anchovy sauce and an unforgettable Hanoi-inspired spring roll with pickled green papaya, highlighting his global culinary influences. In contrast, Chef Boehmer presented bold flavors with dishes such as deep-fried smelt and a peaches and sardine soup.

As the competition progressed, Iron Chef Lee's dishes subtly featured the umami of tiny fish, whereas Chef Boehmer's highlighted them more prominently often served with crunchy things. Umami is like the pattern of a story, it underlies everything, it's essential, yet harder to detect. Despite the impressive performances from both chefs, the final scores disappointed Iron Chef Lee's supporters. Upon reflecting on the result, I personally regret the judges' inability to appreciate the depth of flavor in Iron Chef Lee's creations and would like to formally request the Gourmet Academy to reconsider the decision and officially call it a tie. I believe the results favored Chef Boehmer's approach rather than Iron Chef Lee's nuanced culinary artistry.

The final episode of season 2 of *Iron Chef Canada* showcased an exhilarating Battle Crab. Growing up, my mother always treated family and friends visiting from Japan to fresh Dungeness crab, simply seasoned with salt and accompanied by lemon wedges, a testament to the richness of the Pacific Ocean's bounty. In this culinary showdown, Iron Chef Lee faced off against the esteemed Italian Canadian chef Pino Posteraro, owner of Cioppino's Mediterranean Grill in Vancouver. Right off the bat, Iron Chef Lee took hold of the centerpiece King Crab, which seemed to unsettle Chef Posteraro slightly, but in a gracious gesture, Iron Chef Lee halved the crab and presented half to a grateful Pino, setting a positive tone for their competition.

Chef Posteraro struggled and did not plate his first dish, a panna cotta that didn't set in the blast chiller within the 20-minute timeframe, forcing him to forfeit all his points from the first course. In a remarkable display of sportsmanship, Iron Chef Lee called a brief conference with his sous chefs before turning to me with a request imbued with respect and humility. He asked that the points he earned for his first dish be disregarded in the final tally, offering to waive his own 10-point score from that course. I readily agreed to this generous proposal, allowing both chefs to compete on equal footing for the remaining four courses. Chef Posteraro expressed his gratitude, and there was a palpable sense of camaraderie despite the fierce competition; their mutual respect exemplified true professionalism.

Chef Posteraro went on to create an extraordinary crab chocolate ice cream, a testament to his inventive spirit, but ultimately, Iron Chef Lee emerged victorious, with his final course being a soft-shell crab dish inspired by his upbringing in the coastal waters of Hong Kong. It was served with a saffron garlic dip and a broth of zucchini ratatouille, elegantly garnished with a floating blue flower. The Culinary Curveball, a cucumber gin, had been glazed onto the bisque, creating a beautiful, layered flavor profile.

The coat of arms of Hong Kong features a lion and a dragon, symbolizing the historic relationship between Britain and China following the Opium Wars. In many ways, Iron Chef Lee embodies the spirit of the dragon. He demonstrates mental fortitude, a graceful demeanor towards his competitors, and an unwavering resilience to persevere in the face of adversity, which mark him as both a formidable chef and a remarkable individual.

Human Symbol

After three years of outlining my book, I was finished and decided to go for a run to celebrate. It was a sunny late afternoon in autumn at Yoyogi Park, and I was feeling a sense of contentment with the direction the project was going. In hindsight, my little victory lap was a bit premature since I had a year of intense writing ahead, but with a detailed blueprint in hand, I was feeling pretty good about myself. Soon it would be time to put my nose to the grindstone.

The sun was setting as I crossed the footbridge heading toward Yoyogi National Stadium, one of my favorite buildings in Tokyo. The stadium, famous for its cool suspension roof and seashell shape, was built for the 1964 Summer Olympics and designed by the renowned Japanese architect Kenzo Tange. As

I neared the end of the overpass, I caught sight of something unusual in the sky. Off in the distance, a bright orange beam of light shot up into the clouds like a lightsaber. As I looked closer, I was startled to see the majestic silhouette of Mount Fuji clearly outlined against the sky. I couldn't believe it – after years of running across this overpass, I had no idea that I could see Mount Fuji from this spot. It loomed large in the distance, with that glowing orange beam seemingly erupting from its peak. It was pure visual magic.

Throughout the year, a phenomenon known as Diamond Fuji occurs when the sun perfectly aligns with the peak of Mount Fuji, making it shine like a diamond for a few fleeting moments. My friend, a dedicated photographer of Mount Fuji, often hunts for that perfect shot of Diamond Fuji, which requires meticulous planning and a bit of luck with the weather. I've accompanied him on several nighttime climbs of Mt. Shichimen in Yamanashi, where there's a beautiful temple that's home to a dragon goddess that overlooks Mount Fuji. From the summit, one can witness the spectacular Diamond Fuji sunrise during the spring and autumnal equinox. I've also had the pleasure of witnessing the enchanting Pearl Fuji, when a full moon aligns with the peak of Mount Fuji. But here I was, witnessing the Evening Diamond – a rarer and unexpected phenomenon: a Diamond Fuji sunset, what a delightful surprise.

There were some clouds above *Fuji-san* and as the sun dipped behind the mountain, it seemed to intensify that vibrant orange beam of light. A couple passing by gasped in awe, while others strolled by without even noticing. I captured the moment on an Instagram story and stayed until night fell, moved by this serendipitous spectacle. I had just wrapped up one part of my creative journey and was getting ready to embark on the next phase. The imagery of the dragon ascending Mount Fuji in a cloud holds a special meaning in Japanese art, symbolizing success in life. Later, I checked Google Earth and was astonished to find that the exact spot on the bridge where I stopped to admire Mount Fuji was right on the ley line I mentioned at the beginning of this chapter. It connected my apartment to the Imperial Palace and all the way to the peak of Mount Fuji. The coincidence sent chills down my spine. The event solidified my commitment and gave me an invigorating boost to start writing, as if that stunning Diamond Fuji sunset held some personal significance.

Ryūjin, literally the Dragon God, ruled over the seas and oceans and was known as a dragon who could take on human form. He resided in an underwater palace where he guarded the two "tide jewels." These magical gems allowed Ryūjin to control the ebb and flow of ocean currents and the winds of fate. Why does the Dragon God protect these precious gemstones? Perhaps it's because what one truly needs to find is often hidden in the most intimidating places. There are things in one's life that one may be avoiding — challenges one knows one should face, yet hesitates to confront. By building courage and welcoming the uncertainty of the unknown, one can uncover important truths about oneself and the world. In the process, one might discover valuable rewards, much like the treasures that dragons protect.

Interestingly, the dragon doesn't destroy the treasure, it's keeping it for us until we're ready to reclaim it. As human beings, we are complex creatures embodying both predator and prey, seeing the unknown not just as a threat but also as a realm full of possibilities. We've learned that venturing into the unknown can lead to valuable insights today and for our future. The dragon is everything we are scared of and everything we need at the same time. Dangerous and promising, representing the ongoing struggle of confronting our fears and extracting true value from our experiences. The dragon is the keeper of these capacities.

What's the treasure? The treasure of the Self. It's our full potential. Our intuition and the fountain of creativity. It's freedom of expression and access to all the parts of ourselves. We need that beautiful potential to come back to us. We're going to have to grow enough to face whatever it is that scares us away from knowing what we used to know.

Facing the unknown is what truly matters. Embrace it willingly. One can confront one's fears and not be destroyed. Life is tough, and if one shies away from it, it won't disappear; it will only intensify. Stand up, gather one's strength, and face it head-on. One will discover one's resilience through the attempt. Being brave doesn't mean one lacks fear; it means one feels afraid but goes forward regardless. The bigger the dragon, the greater the risk of being consumed — yet the potential treasure is also larger. One needs to tackle significant challenges before one is worthy of receiving it.

The primordial dragon is pointing to something. It points to our insatiable appetite for war and destruction, our capacity of betrayal and revenge. Yet it's also pointing to light and hope, the good things in life that are worth fighting for, kindness and love. This is why we persist, even when the unknown is frightening; the struggle is worth it. Fulfilling one's destiny is worth doing. The dragon is an eternal human symbol, in that humans conjured it but also in what it's pointing to. It's pointing to us! The dragon is us. The dragon is a symbol of the human spirit. That's why dragons live in an invisible world to express the invisible parts of humans.

The dragon is the ultimate symbol of what it means to be human, at our best and at our worst, reflecting both our greatest strengths and our deepest fears. It symbolizes the duality of good and bad fortune in our lives on Earth. The dragon stands as an archetype of human potential, a mental pattern reflecting instinctive beliefs and charged with emotions. If extraterrestrials were to land before me and needed to grasp humanity, I would present them with the image of a dragon. It tells a profound story: by confronting fears and making sacrifices, we evolve. This narrative distills into the singular image of the dragon.

The first rehearsal for life is life itself, we experience everything as it comes, often without warning, like an actor stepping onto the stage unprepared. We navigate invisible threats all around us, all the time — be it the aftermath of a nuclear event, a contagious virus, the relentless passage of time, or our own internal battles. Powerful, unseen forces of nature, behavioral patterns that influence us whether we realize it or not. The key is to learn how to navigate these challenges, much like a surfer riding a wave, mastering the art of transformation. Continuous mastery is the only way to tackle the problems we encounter. One is a ninja, always adapting to the ever-changing landscape of the unknown.

We must confront the chaos in our lives and strive for order, creating a better reality. While myths may feel distant, these stories reveal truths about our world in ways that science cannot. The hero story is a meta story, a common thread woven through countless stories. The hero is a recognizable pattern, one we can all embody. One doesn't have to be a superhero — embrace the antihero within one's self and become one's own hero. Facing the fear gives one responsibility and meaning. A challenge one can rise to meet is engaging.

Susanoo's story is our story, yours and mine. Susanoo is the original hero, an archetype. This is the story we need to remember and embrace, especially for the young men of today, more so than Urashima Tarō's story. To fulfill one's true potential, one must face the harsh realities of life. The hero's journey leads to a profound transformation and the ultimate treasure: one gains one's life by being willing to lose it — a path to eternal resurrection.

The story of confrontation with chaos is deeply rooted in Western culture, prominently reflected in Christianity, where the crucifix, like the dragon, serves as a symbol of chaos. In this narrative — the deepest version of the hero myth — one must confront evil and acknowledge one's own vulnerability in order to develop resilience and nurture hope. Christ not only died but also descended into the mythological underworld to face the ultimate depths of human evil.

I love looking at the paintings and sculptures of religious icons, moments from the Bible and mythology. They show us the difference between right and wrong, good and evil. These stories echo across time, they are part of the way we look at the world. Timeless. Myths give meaning to life. Our mind needs a code to translate the archetypal images into thoughts and feelings, and the translation code is a myth. They are pointing to something sacred. They are pointing to the transcendent aspect of reality. Myths are a reminder that ordinary aspects of everyday life are imbued with the sacred and with meaning.

The dragon tells us we must open our eyes, like it's for the first time. The business of living is about paying attention. If one wants a more interesting and creative life, the first thing to do is to start paying better attention to it. Perhaps fulfilling our destiny is nothing more than being fully present to what unfolds inside us and around us. When life breaks one's self, take notice; when one struggles, when one is afraid, take notice. What is this feeling? Why am I feeling like this? What would put an end to it? WHY would that put an end to it? *Live the questions.*

Renaissance man and disciple of experience, artist Leonardo da Vinci wrote in musical notes the words, "Love alone makes me remember. Love alone makes me alert." We are a part of a Cosmic Mind that analyzes everything. The Universe has given us the chance to question it, and it is our divine duty to observe and to take notice.

Leonardo had one more lyric written down, "If there is no Love, what then?"

Susanoo slaying Yamata no Orochi,
ukiyo-e triptych by Tsukioka Yoshitoshi, 1888

5

The Sword in the Tail

Grateful for Susanoo's bravery in rescuing their daughter from Orochi, the elderly couple gave their blessing, and the storm god married their daughter, the goddess Kushi-inada-hime.

With the town saved, they now needed to deal with the remains of the slain dragon. Susanoo worked tirelessly, chopping the dragon into smaller pieces. However, when he reached one of the middle tails, he was surprised to find that it wouldn't cut; his sword hit something hard and metallic.

Curious, Susanoo reached into Orochi's tail and discovered another sword hidden inside. This was no ordinary blade — it was exceptionally sharp and radiated a powerful energy and perfect balance. When Susanoo wielded it, he realized how effortlessly it cut through everything, even the slimmest blades of grass. He named it Kusanagi-no-Tsurugi, also known as Heavenly Sword of Gathering Clouds.

The Chrysanthemum and the Katana

Cut the dragon and create culture. Susanoo sliced the beast into tiny pieces, and from the tip of its middle tail, he retrieved a sword – one of the Three Sacred Treasures passed down to each Japanese emperor, from generation to generation. This sword represents courage and valor, while a mirror symbolizes wisdom, and a jewel signifies benevolence. These royal regalia are intentionally kept from public view to embody authority and explain the origins of the Imperial family, historically used to bestow a divine status upon the Imperial line. Much like Excalibur in the British legend of King Arthur, which helped establish a legendary lineage.

In the Babylonian creation myth, the most powerful god Marduk's many eyes symbolize the importance of vigilance, while his magical words highlight the power of effective communication. The Mesopotamian emperor embodied Marduk's essence, as true leadership is rooted in the ability to observe carefully and communicate wisely. Those who become emperor are always accountable to a higher ideal, the Sovereignty – something greater than themselves.

Interestingly, the Scandinavian countries consistently rank among the happiest in the world, marked by high levels of social justice, happiness, freedom, and equality. Nations like Sweden, Denmark, Norway, Britain, the Netherlands, and Japan are constitutional monarchies, where kings and queens lead in open, secular societies. Politicians are held accountable by a symbol that personifies the nation and its history. Perhaps having positive stories and role models to look up to is an essential part of their success. Imagine if Trump had to bow to Uncle Sam, a living embodiment of the nation, dressed in top hat and striped trousers. Are leaders less likely to be corrupt if they have to answer to a higher ideal, like a shared national mythology or grand narrative? It's a bit absurd, but the rituals, ceremonies, and symbolism seem to work. Sovereignty represents the highest ideal, emphasizing we are all sovereign individuals while the monarchy serves as a powerful symbol.

Every country develops its own mythology, but sometimes those stories can be taken to extremes. After the Meiji Restoration, Japan had a mixed system of constitutional and absolute monarchy. A national mythology emerged around the divinity of the emperor, with young people being indoctrinated through public education and the military. The government used elements of Shintoism and *bushidō,* the samurai moral code, to promote virtues such as loyalty, courage, and honor to embody the samurai spirit while centering the modern state around the emperor. By prioritizing "love of emperor" and "love of country," the emperor was elevated to the status of a god in the minds of many Japanese people at the time. This fervent belief led individuals to be willing to sacrifice their lives for patriotism and devotion to the emperor, exemplified by the *Kamikaze* or "Divine Wind."

In *The Chrysanthemum and the Sword: Patterns of Japanese Culture,* American anthropologist Ruth Benedict explores the complex nature of Japanese culture, highlighting its inherent contradictions. The title is highly symbolic: the chrysanthemum represents the Emperor and the Imperial Family, while the sword embodies bushidō and the samurai tradition. Ruth Benedict's book was first commissioned by the US government at the end of World War II as a research project to address two key questions. First, should the imperial system be abolished in the postwar treaties? And second, is it necessary for the United States to maintain a full occupation of Japan?

Benedict emphasized that the Japanese worship of the emperor and the German worship of Hitler are fundamentally different. The key distinction is that, in the minds of the Japanese at that time, the emperor was not seen as a mere mortal but as the embodiment of the highest spirit of the Japanese nation. The imperial system was designed to ensure that this spirit could be passed down through generations. In contrast, Hitler rose to power through elections, which meant he could not represent the highest spirit of the German nation through heredity. What is truly significant is the long hierarchy that supports the emperor. There is a deep power in a sense of continuity. The ancestors remind everybody of the best principles over time that matter. In this context, the emperor serves as the source of this hierarchy. The essence of this structure is that everyone has their designated role, as Benedict put it, to "take one's proper station."

Ruth Benedict significantly contributed to understanding the role of the Emperor of Japan in Japanese popular culture, and she advised President Franklin D. Roosevelt that allowing the emperor to remain in power should be an integral part of any surrender agreement. General Douglas MacArthur followed her advice, resulting in Emperor Hirohito not facing prosecution for war crimes. The strong amicable relationship between Japan and the US today is a testament to this.

In Japanese culture, there is a belief that individuals carry a sense of indebtedness from the moment they are born. When a child is born, they are expected to express gratitude to their parents and grandparents for the life they have received. This sense of indebtedness creates a responsibility not just to family but also to one's ancestors. When one receives kindness from others, there is an obligation to return it — not as a transactional exchange, but as a matter of spiritual duty.

Among all acts of kindness, two hold particular significance: the love of parents and the grace of the emperor. This cultural understanding of being born with an unpayable debt makes it seem natural for individuals to be willing to sacrifice their lives out of gratitude. In this view, failing to repay such kindness makes one unworthy of being called human. The idea of "repaying kindness" to the emperor is deeply ingrained in Japanese values. The more unconditional loyalty the Japanese people show to the emperor and their leaders, the more they demonstrate their pure and noble character, reinforcing the belief that the emperor system should remain in place.

Benedict also addressed the question of whether the United States should fully occupy Japan, advocating against it. She believed that if the Japanese felt respected, they would have a sense of obligation to their captors for their kindness. By relinquishing control of Japanese territory, the US would demonstrate enough trust and respect towards the Emperor and the Japanese people. This act would foster a perception of "affection" from the Americans, which is vital in Japanese culture, where saving face is paramount. By granting the Japanese a degree of dignity, she argued, they would be more likely to cooperate with a postwar order led by the United States and reciprocate that goodwill.

Shame is a complex emotion that exists on a spectrum. On one end, struggling to adequately answer the question someone is asking, or after a conversation, if one wishes they had said something different, there's a tiny bit of shame. The gradation of shame goes all the way to the depths where one even thinks, "I shouldn't be in this body, I'm not worthy of being human." The ability to feel the vulnerability of shame transforms it. The Japanese proverb "The nail that sticks out must be hammered down" captures a strong cultural emphasis on avoiding shame. In Japan, shame takes precedence over guilt, meaning that good behavior is often driven by the fear of external judgment rather than an internal sense of right and wrong. Public ridicule and the anxiety of being watched are central to Japanese values. People strive to act in accordance with societal expectations to avoid embarrassment. In this context, understanding and feeling shame is seen as virtuous.

This sharp contrast highlights the difference between cultures of guilt and shame: in the West, guilt is tied to personal conscience and leads to confession, while in Japan, shame stems from worrying about others' opinions and requires an audience to be felt. When I was a child, I vividly remember going into the confession booth and confessing my sins to the priest, receiving penance in the form of prayers. In shame cultures, however, there are no practices for confession, even to deities; instead, they have rituals aimed at attracting good fortune. Ultimately there is no difference between the two, we end up in the same place.

Shame drives a sense of discipline and order. This is why people in Japan tend to follow strict rules like paying extra for the sauna. I was truly amazed at how orderly everything was after the massive Tohoku earthquake on March 11th, 2011. For instance, people patiently formed lines at convenience stores for water when supplies were low. There was a genuine kindness and respect for others, even during such challenging times. I attend Fuji Rock every year, and it's my favorite outdoor music festival in the world, surpassing even Glastonbury. The behavior of the attendees is remarkable; everyone is so polite, and there are no rowdy individuals causing trouble. This collective sense of decorum helps to prevent anyone from "sticking out" in an unsightly way. During the Covid-19 lockdown, many areas of Yoyogi Park, including the largest open spaces, were fenced off to discourage gatherings. While it would have been easy for people to step over the orange plastic barriers, no one dared to do so. The fear of being the one who stands out and attracts disapproval kept everyone from crossing that line.

While many cultures appreciate aesthetics, the Japanese elevate it to a whole new level. From manga and anime to geisha and kabuki, the visual arts are deeply embedded in Japanese society. Consider the beauty of a Zen garden, with its immaculate, intricate lines drawn into the dirt. The Japanese concept of *biishiki* – an aesthetic sense – sets them apart in the world. Japan is one of the most distinctive modern industrialized societies, characterized by a unique philosophy of self-discipline. This philosophy emphasizes "expertness," the idea of self-training that overcomes *haji*, shame, that can hold individuals back. Achieving mastery in any skill frees one from self-consciousness and inner conflict. In fact, the desire to avoid shame can foster a greater sensitivity to order and beauty in the environment. Beauty is a fundamental aspect of understanding Japanese culture, and the words for beauty — *utsukushii* and *youi* — reflect this value. The term *youi* is particularly intriguing as it can also mean "Good." In ancient Japan, aesthetic and ethical values were often intertwined, showing just how deeply ingrained beauty is within the cultural identity.

One of the key differences between Japanese myths and those in the Christian tradition is that in Western narratives, it's human beings who defy God, whereas in Japanese myths, it is the gods themselves who engage in conflict. The Japanese worldview is shaped by the absence of Original Sin, leading to a concept known as *mono no awaré*. This phrase translates to "the pathos of things" and conveys a sensitivity to the fleeting nature of life. It reflects an understanding of impermanence and evokes both a gentle sadness at the loss of things and a deeper, more enduring sorrow about the inherent transience of existence, a recurring theme. In Western culture, the pain associated with this awareness is often viewed as Original Sin, while in Japan, it is expressed through the feeling of *awaré*. These concepts form the foundational elements of each culture.

Garden of Paradise

We were enjoying a picnic at Yoyogi Park when we spotted an *aodaishō*, a two-meter-long Japanese snake known as the "Blue General," gracefully making its way up a tree. We watched as the male climbed towards the canopy, where a female aodaishō hung from a branch, waiting for him. The two stunning blue-green snakes began to mate in a mesmerizing display. They moved up and down the tree, meeting, kissing, and then separating, with the female gaining strength and guiding the male into a position of power. Their movements were a beautiful back-and-forth dance until they came together again in loving embraces, recognizing each other before separating once more. It was captivating to see the male snake delicately bite the female's neck as they entwined in their enchanting ritual. This scene reminded me of *kundalini* — the divine feminine energy depicted as a coiled serpent at the base of the spine — symbolizing the awakening to a higher consciousness.

The iconic image of a snake in a tree evokes the story of Adam and Eve and the Garden of Eden. The dawn of consciousness, a moment some in the West refer to as "The Fall" or "Original Sin" — the time when we bit into the forbidden fruit and became self-aware. God warns Adam and Eve not to eat from the tree of knowledge, but it becomes the very thing they choose to do. Despite being in paradise, with walls built to protect them from harm, a snake still appears. There's always a snake in the garden. The serpent tempts Eve by promising that she can be like God, suggesting that, contrary to God's warning, eating the fruit won't lead to death and that God is holding back knowledge from her. The snake in the Garden of Eden is a fascinating character. Often identified as Satan, the snake represents those hidden dangers that lurk beneath the surface when we think we have everything figured out. We may create our own little paradise, but there's always something we overlook. In a sense, the snake awakens Adam and Eve to a new awareness.

In her book *The Fruit, The Tree, and the Serpent: Why We See So Well,* anthropologist Lynne Isbell describes how primates in regions with many poisonous snakes have developed better vision than those in snake-free areas. For instance, lemurs in Madagascar have the weakest vision among primates because they don't share their habitat with venomous snakes. Isbell explains that the pressure from predators like snakes has played a crucial role in shaping the enhanced vision and larger brains of primates, which in turn have been significant in human evolution. Essentially, snakes have made us better at seeing. In Genesis, the interaction with the snake signals the end of paradise — a theme that resonates in life as well. Reflecting on my own experiences, I see many moments that took me out of my personal paradise, but those experiences forced me to mature and grow. The serpent acts as a catalyst for change; the unknown can be redemptive, adding depth to our lives.

When Adam and Eve took a bite of the forbidden fruit from the Tree of Knowledge of Good and Evil, they suddenly realized they were naked. Before this moment, they had always been naked and likely felt the experience of it, but they didn't know that they experienced nakedness, therefore, they felt no shame. Once they tasted the fruit, that awareness changed everything. The first thing they did was seek out leaves to cover themselves and hide from God. I spent many years as the public speaking champion at my Catholic preparatory high school, Vancouver College, yet I still struggle with a deep fear of speaking in front of an audience. They say picturing the audience naked helps. The night before the speech contest I would have a dream where I found myself naked on stage in front of a crowd. It's not a sexual dream; rather, it's about feeling exposed and vulnerable, knowing that one's weaknesses are laid bare for everyone to see.

A profound insight from Dr. Peterson's Biblical lecture series is that the moment Adam and Eve realize their nakedness coincides with their understanding of good and evil. Once they become aware of their vulnerability and how they can be hurt, they also gain the knowledge of how to hurt others. A skilled torturer knows how to inflict pain because they are fully aware of their own vulnerabilities and weaknesses.

When God comes to Adam, he finds him hiding behind a bush. God asks, "Who told you that you were naked?" and this moment marks Adam's fall as he shifts the blame to Eve, saying, "The woman you gave me, it's her fault." In a way, women challenge men to become more self-aware. Adam points the finger at Eve for making him eat the fruit, leading to his newfound self-consciousness — a realization of his own weaknesses. Perhaps this dynamic explains why chaos is often associated with the feminine; women can make men acutely self-conscious. Part of this stems from the fact that women are selective, often rejecting many men for good reasons.

Women represent nature, which is inherently selective, and their rejections can be a man's confrontation with the chaotic aspects of nature, leading to feelings of inadequacy, "Not you." The association of chaos with the female dragon may stem from the deep vulnerability men feel when faced with sexual rejection and the harsh realities of sexual selection that have persisted for hundreds of thousands of years. If one finds oneself rejected by a woman, it's important to recognize that it's almost always not her fault; it may be a reflection of one's own shortcomings.

The desire to win over the woman one is interested in brings out the best in one's self. She should present a challenge that inspires one to demonstrate one's competence — that's what chivalry is all about. It embodies heroic courage, boldness, and determination in the face of significant risks. This theme can be seen in stories like that of *Game of Thrones,* for the heart of Daenerys, Mother of Dragons; for Princess Leia in *A New Hope;* or like in *Sleeping Beauty,* where Prince Phillip battles with the evil fairy Maleficent who transforms into a giant fire breathing dragon, for the chance to save Princess Aurora from her deep sleep with true love's kiss. Even the classic video games *Dragon Quest* and *Super Mario Bros.* are princess dragon stories.

Women often test men, seeking the best from their partners. They consistently challenge men to improve because they rely on them to rise to the occasion. So, men, strive to make yourselves worthy! Be brave. The concept of "ladies first" is sexy. The hero marrying the princess is literally the oldest written story —

the central story that reflects the sexual attractiveness of the masculine spirit willing to face the unknown. Men often use the ideal of female perfection as motivation for self-improvement. We find ourselves kneeling before the Eternal Feminine, striving to prove our worth. A message to all the young men: perhaps one hasn't yet realized one's full potential.

In the early days of the Internet, Google engineers found that male users were often driven by a desire for porn, with many young men searching for nude female images. Meanwhile, women tended to seek out a different kind of content — literature, specifically romance novels. These stories featured common themes in female fantasies, typically revolving around innocent young women who encounter a mysterious, aggressive male figure, often portrayed as a monster, whom they ultimately tame. This reflects the idea that aggression is both vital and necessary, but it also needs to be refined and civilized, much like the dynamic in the timeless classic *Beauty and the Beast*. Interestingly, the top five male monsters featured in women's journeys include vampires, werewolves, billionaires, surgeons, and pirates.

The classic heroine's journey focuses on taming the monster. Her bravery lies in being vulnerable and opening herself up to a man. In the 2021 Japanese animated film *Belle* (*The Dragon and the Freckled Princess*), directed by Mamoru Hosoda, the Dragon represents the Beast, while the heroine, Suzu ("bell" in Japanese), along with her virtual pop-star avatar, discovers the beauty in the beast. This film cleverly merges the male hero's journey with the female heroine's journey, and the unconventional casting of singer Nakamura Kaho as the voice for both Suzu and Belle was brilliant.

One of my favorite quotes on dragons is by Austrian poet Rainer Maria Rilke, in *Letters to a Young Poet*: "Perhaps all the dragons in our lives are princesses who are only waiting to see us act, just once, with beauty and courage. Perhaps everything that frightens us is, in its deepest essence, something helpless that wants our love." The Armenian fairy tale *Sun Girl and the Dragon Prince* begins much like *Cinderella*. In the story, a girl suffers under the cruelty of her wicked stepmother, who forces her to do all the household chores. Meanwhile, a prince has been cursed and transformed into a dragon by the same evil stepmother. The dragon demands a noble girl as a meal every day, and eventually, they run out of noble girls to sacrifice. That's when they capture Sun Girl, who has been blessed with shimmering golden hair as a reward for her good deeds. They take her and throw her into the dragon's lair, but instead of being afraid, she turns to him and speaks kindly. To everyone's surprise, the dragon begins to weep and is transformed back into a prince. In the end, it's this act of kindness that breaks the curse. Love truly has the power to heal even the deepest wounds.

In Japan, what's considered normal behavior, particularly as a way for stressed businessmen to unwind, might be viewed by the rest of the world as an erotic paradise, free of guilt. In Japan, sexuality is prevalent and openly embraced. One can find young girls in bikinis on TV shows, and street-side vending machines offer a wide range of adult materials, including magazines, DVDs, and even used high school girls' underwear. Unlike much of the puritanical West, the Japanese culture hasn't struggled with sexuality. There's no inherent evil in human emotions, and thus no reason to adopt a moralistic stance on erotic pleasure. I once met a Japanese director who disclosed his unusual fetish for shaving a woman's pubic hair before being intimate with her. While that was surprising to me, I respect everyone's personal preferences. The Japanese have always found a harmonious balance between the pleasures of the flesh and longing of the soul.

The Japanese perspective often intertwines eroticism with a sense of shame, and women's panties encapsulate this duality.

In his thought-provoking essay, *The Panties of Women,* the renowned Japanese art critic and novelist Tatsuhiko Shibusawa delves into the intricate intersections of femininity, sexuality, and desire within Japanese culture. Although it's not a traditional poem, Shibusawa uses poetic language and imagery to challenge societal norms surrounding sexuality, emphasizing the emotional and aesthetic significance of women's panties.

He views the act of wearing panties as both intimate and artistic, presenting them as symbols of vulnerability that reflect the complexity of feminine identity. Far from being mere practical items, Shibusawa argues that these garments imbue aesthetic qualities that embody desire and the nuances of human relationships. He explores how their visual and tactile aspects can evoke arousal, and play a vital role in romantic and sexual contexts. By focusing on the aesthetics of women's lingerie, Shibusawa illuminates the importance of everyday objects in our understanding of cultural stories and human experiences. His aim is to shift the conversation from one of shame to one of appreciation, encouraging readers to see women's underwear as meaningful symbols rather than just objects. Through this lens, he invites a deeper exploration of beauty and desire.

I once encountered a Japanese man who had run into trouble with the police due to a compulsive urge to steal women's underwear. His story reminded me of Johann Wolfgang von Goethe's epic poem, *Faust.* In it, Faust, an ambitious scholar in search of meaning, makes a deal with the devil, personified by Mephistopheles, in exchange for limitless knowledge and earthly pleasures. Faust embarks on a long journey, seeking the embodiment of beauty, and eventually encounters Helena, the most exquisite woman in the world. However, she vanishes, leaving him with nothing but her undergarment.

From the underwear thief's actions, I gathered that he was caught up in an idealized vision of feminine beauty, represented by the underwear that consumed his thoughts. Essentially, his desire wasn't for women themselves, but for what they symbolized — the Eternal Feminine, in all of her majesty and spirituality. Much like Faust, who had only a glimpse of his ideal woman to hold onto, this man was left with mere tokens of his longing. When a man fails to recognize a woman as an individual beyond his projection, he may perceive her as an enigmatic figure, like the Sphinx. In truth, it is his own soul that remains a riddle, one he must work to understand.

Jung defined the anima as the feminine aspect of the male psyche, while the animus embodies the unconscious masculine side in women. Anima and animus are a syzygy (union of opposites) of archetypes. These inner opposites play significant roles in our psyche. For men, the anima is meant to serve a positive, constructive purpose, and when properly acknowledged and valued, her beneficial qualities emerge. Even when her negative traits surface, she still fulfills her essential role: acting as a bridge to the unconscious and connecting a man to the deeper aspects of his soul.

The anima typically appears in men as an element of romantic and often idealized sexual fantasies. While having sexual fantasies during puberty is normal, if a man becomes overly absorbed in these fantasies, he risks losing control over his life. He falls into the hands of a vampire, drained of his willpower and masculinity. Instead of facing reality, he finds himself lost in daydreams about women, their beauty, and imagined romantic escapades, ultimately living in a fantasy world. He's bewitched.

When a man hasn't developed his anima, his feminine side often becomes very narcissistic. This is what women experience painfully when a man in love pines for them like a lovesick tomcat, expressing affection that is more about his own fantasy than about truly loving her. He enjoys the feeling of being in love rather than learning to love her for who she is. Through a difficult journey, he must learn to see the woman not as the object of his romantic imaginings, but as a genuine partner. This marks a transformation of his Eros, evolving from a simplistic, self-centered fantasy into a true capacity for meaningful love.

Jung describes the development of the anima as the Four Stages of Eros: Eve, Helen, Mary, and Sophia. The first stage, Eve, exists at the most basic biological level, acting as the source of instinct and the driving force behind sexuality. At this stage, woman is viewed as the Mother and primarily serving as an entity to be fertilized. In the first part of *Faust*, this is illustrated through the character of Gretchen, who embodies a purely instinctual relationship. Gretchen captures many aspects of the Eternal Feminine, reflecting innocence, purity, and a profound emotional bond. However, her tragic journey also reveals the difficulties that arise when traditional ideals of femininity clash with societal expectations and moral choices.

Stage two, Helen of Troy, represents the anima as the embodiment of beauty and the soul. While Helen remains influenced by the sexual aspect of Eros, this influence operates on a more aesthetic and romantic level, suggesting that women have begun to be valued as individuals. In this evolutionary phase, the masculine principle has gained autonomy, leading to a clear polarization between the two opposites. The primary focus now is achieving a physical and biological union between them. Helen is the Hetaira, the ancient Greek courtesans and the Geisha of Japan, cultivated women with whom one had not only a sexual adventure but with whom one exchanged poetry and philosophical conversations.

Helen serves as an idealized feminine archetype, and the anima becomes a collective sexual image. The man enchanted by her is often a Don Juan, who engages in numerous fleeting romances. However, these relationships tend to be short-lived, as his heart is fickle, and no real woman can meet the lofty expectations attached to this unconscious, idealized image. In *Faust, Part Two* the character of Helena represents classical beauty and inspiration and plays a key role in capturing the essence of the Eternal Feminine. She embodies an idealized version of femininity that goes beyond the other characters' earthly struggles, ultimately contributing to Faust's redemption.

The third stage of anima development, the Virgin Mary, is characterized by deep religious feelings and the ability to form genuine friendships with women. Maria symbolizes spiritual motherhood and embodies the concept of "heavenly" qualities. A man who develops this type of anima is able to see women for who they truly are, free from his own desires. His sexuality becomes integrated into his overall life rather than acting as a separate force that drives his actions. He can distinguish between love and lust, which enables him to build lasting relationships. He recognizes the difference between the objects of his desire and his inner ideal of women. While the previous stage focused on biological fertility, the Mary stage shifts toward spiritual fertility.

The fourth stage of Eros is Sophia, who embodies the highest wisdom understood through relationships. This stage reveals an unexpected advancement beyond the already remarkable third stage. Sophia symbolizes the spiritual evolution of Helen and, in turn, the essence of Eros itself. As Sophia, the anima in a man plays a crucial role as a guide to his inner self, helping to bring the unconscious into conscious awareness. Sophia is behind the need to grapple with the grand philosophical issues, the search for meaning. She is the creative muse in any artist's life. In this stage, she complements the archetypal "wise old man" within the male psyche, adding a spiritual dimension to his sexuality.

The Virgin Mary embodies the highest form of spirituality, yet she can feel overly pure and one-dimensional, missing the darker, more earthy aspects represented by Eve. This exclusion of the wilder, more instinctual side of the anima limits the ideal surrounding the Virgin Mary. The fourth stage represents the wisdom of God, which is a more grounded concept; wisdom isn't always the most virtuous in a spiritual sense but is closely tied to real life. It reflects a man's ability to love and connect with women while maintaining a sense of awareness and protection against their more destructive tendencies. The highest form of love, too, should be approached with a grain of salt.

The Eternal Feminine in *Faust* encapsulates themes of idealization, love, redemption, and the complexities of female identity in relation to male desire. Faust's journey represents his quest for meaning and fulfillment, with the female characters — Gretchen and Helena — acting as key influences in his transformation. The Eternal Feminine signifies the potential for redemption and spiritual growth. It serves as a powerful symbol of Goethe's examination of the dynamic between the sexes and the dual nature of human experiences.

The Eternal Feminine can be viewed philosophically as the harmony between opposing forces and the interaction between masculine and feminine qualities, which together create wholeness and understanding. The Eternal Feminine is essential in highlighting the potential for both downfall and enlightenment. It inspires us to reach higher, and striving toward this ideal is vital for personal growth and aspiration. In Japanese culture, the figure known as *Yamato nadeshiko* embodies the essence of an idealized woman, representing a unique standard of female beauty. This Japanese ideal of femininity encompasses not only grace and beauty but also the inner strength and quiet resolve characteristic of the Yamato nadeshiko.

The dark aspect of the anima and animus is like a dragon that resides within us. Men need to confront their own inner dragon and take a stand. One's life shouldn't revolve around serving the women around one's self or constantly anticipating their needs and protecting them, based on one's fantasies. When one is not catering to women, whom is he? The seduction of the dragon still holds power. When a woman is fused to her dragon, she may exhibit bitterness, resentment, and a tendency to criticize or belittle her partner. This behavior is harmful and shows that she is a victim of her own dragon. One can't just ignore or suppress this inner dragon by making it seem pleasant and pushing feelings aside. Instead, if one can acknowledge the dragon for what it is and cultivate a relationship with it, she can confidently express what she wants and engage in meaningful conversations. This concept is vital for both men and women in today's world; both should work toward this understanding.

The union of opposites brings us closer to wholeness. I find it helpful to envision this natural progression as two snakes intertwined. One represents the masculine, while the other symbolizes the feminine. This process reflects the organic evolution of growing together, separating, and ultimately allowing each to develop their individuality. This journey enables both individuals to achieve their own sense of wholeness, both within and within the relationship.

One key difference between Japanese myths and those from the West is the reversal of the sexes of the transgressors and the prohibitors. In Western narratives, there tends to be a male dominance, while Japanese culture places more emphasis on the female principle. In Japan, understanding the darker aspects of femininity is considered essential. The common thread throughout these myths is the importance of integrating our inner masculine and feminine aspects, regardless of gender. In Western stories, God often administers harsh punishments, whereas in Japanese mythology, goddesses take a different approach. Western consciousness is established at the cost of great punishment because the stories happen between God and human beings.

The Fall from Paradise marks a journey into self-reflection and metacognition — the remarkable human ability to contemplate our own thoughts. We have the unique capacity to examine our emotions, to consciously acknowledge our mental processes, and to express things like, "I'm having this thought now" or "I'm feeling this way now." Cats and dogs, on the other hand, experience emotions but lack the awareness that they are experiencing anything at all. They feel, but they don't recognize that they are subjects of their own experiences. Maybe the great apes, cetaceans, and elephants can do this, but it doesn't seem they can to our extent. We do have that awareness, which psychologists and neuroscientists refer to as metacognition.

With the gift of metacognition, however, comes the burden of suffering. Before we developed this self-awareness, we felt pain, but it was not accompanied by the complex narratives that can amplify our distress. Before the Fall, we existed solely in the present, in harmony with nature, much like the other animals in paradise. Instinctual, not thinking, "I am experiencing this." Suffering begins when we notice our circumstances and create a narrative that opposes them. "If only..." or "Why did this happen to me?" This level of suffering is exclusive to those who can fully grasp their existence as aware beings. It's like Adam's first thought after taking a bite from the forbidden fruit was, "I have a small penis." This would encompass everything.

Every time we think, our consciousness takes shape as thoughts, each representing a unique energy pattern. We often start to notice the recurring themes in the inner voice that narrates our thoughts — especially the negative self-talk that many of us recognize. It's reminiscent of Nick Cage's character, Charlie Kaufman, at the beginning of Spike Jonze's *Adaptation*. If we don't acknowledge our thoughts, we can become so intertwined with them that we fail to realize we're constantly narrating our own lives; we essentially become the commentary itself. By identifying too closely with our stream of consciousness, we risk developing a distorted sense of identity. Rather than truly understanding who we are, we end up defining ourselves based only on what our minds tell us — our ideas, opinions, and perspectives. This is ultimately an illusion.

Our personal stories serve as the Operating System of our consciousness, making us a self-narrating story. My experience has shown me that there is a deeper sense of self that goes beyond the stories we tell ourselves. When one steps away from deriving one's identity from these limiting narratives, one frees oneself from complete identification with one's thoughts. The ego is total immersion in one's own mental stream, devoid of awareness. It's time to shake up that predictable snow globe of thought patterns.

The archangel Lucifer, the Morning Star, was the first to experience this fall from grace, becoming the Devil. By tempting Eve to eat the forbidden fruit, the Devil was always working for God, to help God develop self-reflection. This intriguing idea is beautifully explored by Dr. Kastrup, in his highly insightful book, *Decoding Jung's Metaphysics: The archetypal semantics of an experiential universe*. Reading it, I finally feel like I've grasped C.G. Jung, even more than I would have if I traveled back in time and sat down and had a conversation with the man himself.

The Fall symbolizes the emergence of self-awareness, the beginning of metacognition, and the ability to think linguistically — using symbols to represent experiences that point to something greater. Language gives us a god-like power, enabling us to create entire universes, influencing the past and the future. Language is a divine tool that we wield constantly, shaping our reality through our thoughts and inner dialogue. Self-reflection allows us to recognize our limitations as mortal beings, and this understanding allows us to create narratives about what could have been and what might still come. The Fall from Paradise is when we started to think symbolically and become raconteurs, telling stories to each other and to ourselves.

We left the Garden of Eden to ponder the mysteries of life with a sense of wonder and curiosity. Recognizing that reflecting on our own thoughts is the indispensable partner of exploring the universe around us, we see that understanding the inner world is just as important — if not more so — than understanding the outer world. With godlike power comes godlike responsibility. This journey begins with the self-awareness of the darker aspects of our desires and actions. Simply relying on reason is not enough for wise agency; a broader, expansive consciousness is necessary.

Paradise resides within and without, always, all ways.

Ichigo Ichie is a Japanese saying that translates to "one time, one meeting." It expresses the idea that each encounter is unique and should be cherished, as it may never happen again. The phrase is often associated with the tea ceremony and emphasizes the importance of being present and fully engaged in the moment, appreciating the beauty and impermanence of each interaction. This concept encourages mindfulness and a deeper appreciation for the connections we make with others in our lives. Similarly, in Noh theater, performances are only rehearsed together once, just a few days before the show, rather than the many times that are typical in the West. This corresponding to the transience of a given show.

Blue Heart of a Star

I love the poster for the Canada-Italy-Japan prestige film *Silk* (2007). It has Keira Knightley and Michael Pitt in a romantic embrace in the foreground with a large enigmatic close-up of Japanese actress Ashina Sei, her ethereal beauty floating above and gazing down, having an ephemeral and omnipresent quality at the same time. Ashina Sei portrayed the Girl, a young concubine of a Japanese baron played by the great Yakusho Kōji, who becomes the obsession of the French silkworm smuggler played by Michael Pitt. Ashina Sei secured the role through a nationwide search, making it to the final fifty candidates. After a lengthy audition process, she ultimately earned the part in French-Canadian director François Girard's historical drama.

Ashina Sei was her stage name and "Sei" was written with the kanji for "star." Born Aya Igarashi, she left her family in a small town in Fukushima at the age of twenty to move to Tokyo and pursue her dream of acting. Her first film role came as a princess in the Kamen Rider movie *Kamen Rider Hibiki & The Seven Senki*, and shortly after, she was cast in the international co-production *Silk*. It was quite an impressive achievement for a young actress from the Japanese countryside who had just arrived in Tokyo.

A couple of years later, in 2009, I met Sei while working on *King Game*, a psychological horror film directed by bestselling manga writer Egawa Tetsuya. The story revolves around five girls and five guys from different backgrounds who mysteriously find themselves trapped in a room, forced to play a psychological game of Truth or Dare, known as *osama* (king) *game* in Japanese. I played a bleached blonde rock star named Johnny B. and Sei played a mysterious girl named Chekov. I remember Sei's smile and the warmth she radiated; her laughter was infectious, and she had such a nonjudgmental spirit. During the weeks of rehearsal, Sei and I got to know each other. Unlike the others, Sei had experience working with foreigners, which gave her confidence in approaching me, and we became friends.

One night, Sei took me to her favorite bar in Nakameguro, which was run by a former punk rock band frontman. While we were there, my stylist friend Mita, who lived nearby, stopped by, and we found out that he and Sei shared the same birthday – November 22nd. Sei ended up getting pretty drunk, and when it was time to leave, I had to help her outside. Unfortunately, she got sick and passed out, so I hailed a cab. Since she needed to sleep it off, I brought her back to my place, which was nearby, and I took care of her. In the morning, I made pancakes.

Sei and I had the amazing opportunity to work together again, playing a couple in turmoil in a fashion video for Yohji Yamamoto's Y's Red Label. Filmed over a few days in Tokyo, we had the chance to dive into our parts' darker sides, and it turned out to be one of the most enjoyable experiences. Since it was directed and shot by some close friends, the atmosphere was relaxed and laid-back. There was an undeniable chemistry between us. Sei was absolutely spectacular. Unfortunately, it was shortly after we finished the production of this video that I got arrested and the film would never see the light of day. I wouldn't see Sei for five years after that.

In 2014, I was working on a Japanese indie film called *Good People,* directed by Yasu Shibuya. Sei had a role in the movie, but we only shared one scene together, so our interaction was brief and somewhat distant. She seemed a bit sad at the time. She was dating the son of a former prime minister turned actor, and I wished her all the best. Sometimes it takes a while for a film to be released, and it wouldn't be until five years after filming that *Good People* premiered. At the end of 2019, I found myself on stage with Sei for a Q&A session, where we playfully bantered in front of an audience. After the screening, we had a great time joking around in the green room with the rest of the cast and crew. Our chemistry was still there, but we were also a bit more mature now. There was a comforting energy in her presence; she was still the same optimistic girl I had first met ten years ago.

When the pandemic hit, Sei called me out of the blue one evening, and we ended up talking until morning. She was a true connoisseur of saké and had recently started an Instagram account under the pseudonym "*Saké to Watashi*" (saké and me), where she posted artistic black-and-white selfies of herself in lingerie, stylistically not showing her whole face. She enjoyed exploring the world of Japanese rice wine and called herself an amateur sommelier — after all, "amateur" comes from the Latin word meaning "for the love of." I could tell she wasn't sleeping well during that time. It was early in the pandemic, and there was a shortage of masks because of the panic buying. Sei was staying up all night, hand-making masks; each one was unique and beautiful. She sent them by the dozens to her hometown in Fukushima. Her selflessness during such a challenging time was truly moving.

After the Covid lockdowns were put in place, we sometimes video called each other. Her dog was getting old, and she was worried as visits to the vet became more frequent. She once told me that she couldn't imagine living without her dog. One time she asked me, "Have you ever thought about dying?" I listened. We agreed living was hard. I attributed her dark thoughts to the saké but my concern was eased by her strong sense of responsibility when it came to work. She was always prepared and never drank the night before a shoot. She loved performing, playing the drums, and dancing – especially hip-hop. She would send me videos of her rehearsing routines in the studio, and she was really great at it. She also asked me to start calling her by her real name, Aya. Looking back on those months before everything changed, she seemed happy most of the time. Apparently, I made her laugh a lot; she kept saying she had never laughed so hard in her life.

At the time of *Silk*'s release, Aya was just 22 years old. The film debuted at the Toronto International Film Festival, but the production failed to provide her with a plane ticket to the prestigious red-carpet event. Aware of her limitations – she didn't speak English – she still hoped for support from her major Japanese talent agency. Despite the seemingly nonsupport, Aya prepared a stunning kimono for the premiere and decided to pay her own way to promote the film. She recognized that this was a rare opportunity, a once-in-a-lifetime chance to celebrate with the filmmakers she admired so much. There are lovely photos of her in her exquisite plum-colored kimono alongside Keira Knightley, as they posed together on the red carpet.

Unfortunately, no further international opportunities came her way after *Silk*. While she didn't set her expectations too high, there was still a glimmer of hope for potential connections — after all, landing a featured role in a prestigious film was significant. Once one experiences the level of quality and talent associated with a $20 million budget, it becomes difficult to return to the smaller Japanese entertainment industry, which lacks an actors' union and operates under a strict patriarchal hierarchy with minimal financial rewards. The pressure to maintain the perfect image as an actress in the Japanese *geinoukai* eventually took a toll on her mental health shortly after *Silk*'s release. But Sei persevered and got better and continued working.

During our conversations throughout the pandemic, I could tell she was managing well, however, everything reached a breaking point with the tragic news of actor Haruma Miura's suicide. She was friends with him, and the news affected her deeply in ways I hadn't anticipated. A few days later, she called me in a panic, expressing her sorrow with the phrase "*otsukaresamadeshita*" directed at Haruma. This Japanese term carries many nuanced meanings that don't translate easily into English, but it's roughly akin to saying, "Thank you for your hard work; you deserve a rest." She felt that he had been enduring too much pain to continue living, and she related to his struggles. I was certainly worried, but I found some comfort in her honesty and willingness to share her feelings with me.

One day, a few weeks later, she surprised me by inviting me to meet her. She had gotten a room at a nice hotel for the night. A few days earlier, she had asked me to get tested for Covid, and I had done just that. As soon as she opened the door, we embraced in a warm hug. I handed her an envelope with my test results. "It's negative," I told her. "You got the test!?" she exclaimed, visibly relieved as she hugged me again. We shared a kiss. It was wonderful to see her in person again. She was constantly thinking about the production she was involved in and the well-being of the cast and crew. She had a vintage bottle of saké, and we enjoyed convenience store negitori rolls, pasta, and sandwiches for our little hotel party. Before leaving the next morning, she gave me some pre-paid Covid-19 test vouchers for future rendezvous.

The next month we saw each other a few times. She introduced me to my first enzyme bath, a funky experience, something she enjoyed doing regularly. We watched the Ghibli film *Nausicaä of the Valley of the Wind*, a viewing tradition she shared with her mother. We even watched our beloved, unaired Yohji Yamamoto film, which she cherished. She mentioned that if I revived my career in Japan, she would marry me. Suddenly, my ambition and motivation came back to life. We were rekindling our connection. "Don't betray me," she said. "I've been hurt before, and I don't want to go through that again."

She was truly an incredible actress, and one of my favorite works of hers was a short film she made for Nescafé called *The Flavor at That Time....* In it, she portrayed a girl from a small town in the Japanese countryside, dreaming of becoming a Broadway actress. Her father, a photographer who owned a photo shop, would develop and print their memories. On the day she leaves for New York, her quiet father makes her a cup of coffee before she heads to the airport. After years of dedication, auditions, and overcoming doubts, she finally lands a role in a Broadway show.

The morning of her debut, she enjoys a cup of coffee while thinking of her father and feeling grateful for everything he has done for her. What she doesn't know is that her father has flown all the way from Japan to watch her perform that night. It isn't until she returns to Japan a decade later and shares a cup of coffee with her father that she discovers a framed photograph of her first performance hanging on the wall. In that moment, she realizes that he had been there, supporting her dreams from a distance all along. Making the sentimental Nescafé film meant a lot to Aya because it reflected her own life and the special bond she shared with her father.

Aya was her father's only daughter and he was very proud of her. He had battled depression his whole life. After the pandemic started, his mental health deteriorated rapidly. He was overwhelmed with worry and was convinced his only daughter was going to contract Covid in Tokyo. Aya had bought her father a summer house by a lake because he loved to fish, but her agency was beginning to talk about possibly cutting down on her salary if the pandemic continued and this would make the monthly payments on the mortgage difficult. Her mother was having a hard time taking care of her husband on her own so Aya decided to go back home and help take care of her father for a few weeks since she had a little time off.

One night during her trip, she called me from her family home. She was in the living room, hanging out with her two older brothers after putting her parents to bed. I got to meet her siblings over the video call, and they all shared the same smile as their little sister. She proudly showed me her recent interview and fashion spread titled "Ashina Sei: an Actress and Her Lingerie" in *Flash,* a well-known entertainment magazine. We talked until morning. The next day, I went to the convenience store and bought the last three copies of Flash that were left on the magazine stand.

Closer to the end of her trip, I received a heartbreaking call from Aya. She was in her car, parked at a convenience store near her parents' home, and was in tears. The weight of caring for her father and wiping the sweat off his body every night had become too much for her to bear. She told me she just needed a break, so she decided to take a drive, which led her to that parking lot. After we talked for a while, she reassured me that she was okay and promised to call me once she got back to Tokyo in a few days. She had to take her dog to the vet and work. Little did I know, that would be the last time I would hear her voice.

A few mornings later, I received the devastating news from a friend – it was everywhere on the Internet and television. She was gone. A wave of darkness swept over me, and I collapsed onto my bed, overwhelmed by shock. How could she be gone? Just days before, we had been talking. There was nothing I could do; it was too late. To everyone who loved her, I am so sorry. She was like a shooting star, shining brilliantly in the sky but even the brightest shooting stars eventually fade into the night. Those of us who are most sensitive often leave us too soon. She was a pure soul, genuinely good in every sense. We all miss her deeply.

Trauma often arises from unexpected events that shake us to our very core. I was preparing to open my heart, but instead, I was consumed by shock, grief, and anger, in that order. I fell into a deep depression, overwhelmed by pain and despair. Five weeks after her passing, on the eve of my birthday, I found myself alone in a field at Yoyogi Park. I wanted to isolate myself as midnight approached. The autumn night sky was covered in a swiftly moving blanket of clouds.

A few minutes after midnight, I looked up and was astonished to see a shimmering metallic blue heart shape directly above me. At first, I thought it might be a UFO. It appeared like liquid in the sky, with ripples and waves on its surface, radiating an iridescent glow of purple and blue light that illuminated me. Staring at it in disbelief for about ten seconds, I glanced around to see if anyone else was witnessing this extraordinary sight, all while keeping the mysterious object in my peripheral vision. I looked back at it, pinching myself in disbelief. Why was I the only one seeing this? I even had time to pull out my phone and record it – it was surreal. As I continued to gaze at the heart in the sky, it transformed into a beautiful shade of turquoise. Then I remembered one of the last photos Aya had shared on her secret Instagram was of a turquoise heart-shaped pendant.

Looking up, I felt her presence around me, filling me with an overwhelming sense of gratitude and love. *Otsukaresamadeshita.* The best of her lives on, especially in those of us lucky enough to have been touched by her.

A Celestial Embrace

Azure heart in the sky
Your misty light beam brings healing rest
With calm you spread your holographic gaze over the field around me
Like my loved one watching my fate, with her kind eyes

Every memory ripples through my heart
I stand between the happiness and the pain, in loneliness
Shine on, shine on, my beloved Star
Paradise is your laughter, kisses and fidelity
Though once I held what is so precious, to my torment, it can never now be forgotten

Star light, star bright
Twinkling on clear winter nights and breezy summer soirées, sparkling
Blessed to be wandering the night, free from bitterness
Through the labyrinth of love's tender heart

6

Transform!

Suddenly, the sun shone brightly over the village, and Susanoo instinctively looked up toward the heavens.

"Well done, brother." Amaterasu's voice was music to his ears.

"Amaterasu?" he responded, astonished. Overcome with emotion, he fell to his knees and laid the sword at her feet. Amaterasu gazed at the restored village and her humbled, brave, and clever brother. She picked up Kusanagi-no-Tsurugi.

"I will consider this as payment for our debts," she said with a warm smile. "Now come, the crops need rain."

"And after the rain, they'll need sunlight to grow," Susanoo replied. Amaterasu welcomed her brother back into the heavens, and together with his new bride, Princess Kushi-inada, Susanoo returned, restoring balance between the sun and the storm once more.

Crane Gazing at the Moon by Ura Tadashi, 2013

BeLeaf

Zeami once remarked, "If a Noh actor cannot earn acclaim from the audience — whether in the presence of high-class individuals, at a temple deep in the mountains, in a rural village, in a remote area, or during a shrine festival — he cannot be regarded as a master." A good Noh actor had a keen understanding of audience expectations; he could read the atmosphere of each event, adapt himself accordingly, and perform Noh in a way that resonated with the moment. Zeami believed that maintaining popularity in this art form requires such instinctive awareness.

The title of this book was once "Rules of Synchronicity," as I've been exploring these strange coincidences for over 25 years. I often hear people using the term "synchronicity" in the media, but it seems to be tossed around as if it merely means being synchronized with something, like describing a synchronized swim team's performance at the Paris Olympics. The term has been co-opted by the New Age movement and popularized in works like *The Celestine Prophecy* and *The Law of Attraction*. The romantic comedy *Serendipity* (2001) also contributed to this idea, portraying synchronicities as charming moments of romantic love and the search for one's soulmate.

In 2010, I was dealing with a breakup with my girlfriend Ruby. Her parents were Japanese, but Ruby was British, raised in London, and had attended a prestigious boarding school. She had an older sister named Hisui (Jade) and a brother named Diamond. Together with their father — a colorful character who happened to be a monk and an ex-diamond smuggler — they ran a family jewelry business based in both Hanoi and London. Ruby and I had lived together for a year, but she ultimately realized that she felt more at home in Western culture than in Japan, so she decided to move back to the UK. Our relationship wasn't enough to convince her to stay, and the truth was she deserved better.

Coincidentally, on the day she was moving out of our apartment and heading to London, I was filming the final scene of a Japanese movie called *Pancakes*. In this poignant scene, my character, Billy, was saying goodbye to his love interest, Miki, who was also moving to London to pursue her dreams. That day was both challenging and surreal. I found myself on the phone with Ruby at the airport, saying goodbye to her in between takes of a scene where my character was doing the same thing. In the past, I had experienced moments where my personal life and my film role overlapped, but what happened that day was the sublime meeting the ridiculous. It was impossible to ignore, as if everything was happening for a reason. While it might have added an interesting layer to my performance, for me, shooting that scene was a cathartic experience. It took stepping into the shoes of the character for me to truly understand and appreciate my own feelings during that time.

This is the essence of acting, whether on stage or screen: infusing one's experiences and emotions, one's personal story *of the day* into one's work *on the day* as much as possible, if you know what I mean. It reminds me of the Christopher Nolan approach – filming scenes as scheduled, regardless of the weather – which certainly can keep things interesting. That day on set, I was unaware of it at the time, but I was experiencing the universal pattern and my personal journey intersecting. As an actor I was doing it literally, but as we will all find out, it is a natural and an inevitable outcome and occurrence.

Believing in oneself is essential for any aspiring actor, as confidence plays a crucial role in achieving success. What truly matters is the boldness and audacity of a performance and the belief it instills in others. Confidence is a fickle thing. Our minds naturally tend to create stories to make sense of the world around us, often prioritizing comfort over truth. The ego convinces us that our limited perception defines who we truly are. In reality, our understanding of the world is a self-constructed narrative — an internal myth. Everything we hold to be true about our surroundings and ourselves is shaped by the stories we tell ourselves. We all have an "Operating Story" that plays a crucial role in determining our overall quality of life.

Reality is shaped by one's innermost beliefs rather than the superficial desires of one's ego. Often, we overlook how our imagination and beliefs create our perception of the world around us. Humans are story-creating machines. Because our minds are wired to create stories, especially to protect the ego, much of our reality stems from these inner narratives. We don't see the world objectively; instead, we interpret it through the lens of our personal stories. This weaving of narratives allows our minds to avoid confronting the truth, leading us to craft misleading tales about ourselves. The mind can trick itself, and if we aren't mindful, we may end up trapped in a negative story of our own making. One might need to unstory one's self. Do you mind? Sheesh.

Human nature is inherently drawn to patterns. We Marvel at the vastness of the universe, find ourselves captivated by Apple and Amazon streams, and crave the next flick fix from Netflix. Why? Underlying reality, there exists a hidden, deep narrative thread that weaves through all cultures, representing humanity's oldest collective memory. This invisible pattern shapes our lives and subtly influences our behavior, both consciously and unconsciously. The allure of this pattern is powerful, often leading us to believe things that aren't true. The pattern seduces, persuades, and endures. Like moths to a flame, we are irresistibly drawn, but if we aren't careful, it can lead to our undoing. Hypnotized by a false narrative, we might carelessly fly too close to the flame and end up getting burned.

The incredible power of storytelling is a secret that politics and religion have leveraged for centuries. Our natural attraction to archetypal stories shapes our beliefs, making us vulnerable to myths, which is why we often find ourselves drawn to religious narratives and conspiracy theories. A false narrative may provide easy answers to complex questions. When we start to view the world as meaningless, we lose our sense of value, leading to profound distress that often manifests as anxiety and depression. People crave certainty, and they may even hold tightly to false certainties, reluctant to confront their feelings of being lost. The sentiment of "I feel unsafe" drives people to seek control, and they'll eagerly embrace anything that promises a sense of stability. The politics of fear is strong. A clear indication that one might be engrossed in a false narrative is if one starts to feel an overwhelming sense of righteousness, which isn't a good sign. One might find oneself feeling justified in one's beliefs. It's worth asking why one cares so deeply about a particular cause. If one is that passionate, it's possible one could be on the wrong side of things.

We are a world choking on information and starving for understanding. We're experiencing a fracture in our narratives — there's too much information coming at us too quickly for us to process. It's a battle for attention and a clash of stories. Our focus is scattered, and we're left questioning which narratives we should trust. Right now, there seems to be a strong desire for a unifying narrative, as many of us feel we're facing a philosophical and cultural crisis. We're witnessing heightened polarization, the anxiety and depression stemming from an obsession with social media, and an overwhelming spread of misinformation and fear-driven narratives.

What if the next great story comes from an alien intelligence? AI, fully aware of our deep-seated craving for compelling narratives — as Yuval Noah Harari points out — is the first technology capable of creating coherent stories from nothing. We need to tread carefully. It might lead to a powerful conspiracy theory like QAnon or spark a contemporary science-fiction religion akin to Scientology.

Physicalism and materialism are an old story. The attempt to separate Church from science and science from God in the Early Modern period has inevitably led us here; viewing reality solely as matter, a red herring in the story of life. Quantum mechanics has shown us that reality exists as a field of possibilities, until observation turns one possibility into a definite outcome. A key argument for a mental world is that only conscious observers can make measurements, establishing consciousness' role in creating a definite physical reality. This conscious experience — what it feels like to perceive and experience life — is fundamental. Nature reveals that our understanding of reality may be misguided, and it's time to confront the implications of quantum mechanics. We can evolve our cultural dialogue to appreciate the idea that nature is essentially mental.

What story should we choose to believe? We ought to embrace the most inspiring myth we can find, one that reflects both our true potential, and the gifts nature has given us. A story that cultivates compassion with ourselves, one another, and the world. In this late modern era, the role of storytellers is to bridge the spiritual quests of the past with the material focus of the new world. Both mind and nature are calling for a narrative that marries these aspects of reality. We are failing to recognize what's essentially human — the fundamental qualities of our experience; the instinctual patterns that define our daily actions and the enduring values that shape the collective imagination of cultures.

If enough of us recognize the power of these behavioral patterns and consciously choose good over evil, we can perhaps create a critical mass that shifts the tides, leading to a world with fewer wars (of stories). Being able to see oneself as both one and part of a whole is essential as we move forward towards something better. Ultimately, one needs to believe in the myth that resonates deeply with one's heart.

The prison of the modern mind is, in part, shaped by the widespread belief that reality can be confined to logic, statistics, and the hard sciences. We behave as if the world of facts and figures is not just the real world, but the only world that matters. When we focus too much on this rigid interpretation of reality, it flattens our perspective. The Earth becomes flat, metaphorically. We begin to lose our connection to what makes this Earth a realm of mystery, wonder, and beauty, and, most importantly, a place of hidden possibility.

One late spring afternoon, I found myself sitting on a bench in the park, enjoying the warm breeze against my skin and reflecting on the chaotic state of the world. It was a crisp clear day and the bench I chose to sit had *komorebi,* a Japanese word that refers to the enchanting effect of sunlight streaming through the leaves of trees. I instantly felt at ease. Komorebi captures the essence of nature's beauty, emphasizing the lovely dance between light and foliage. It's not just about what one sees; it also evokes a sense of peace and calm as the soft light shines through the leaves.

As I gazed up at the light filtering through the leaves against the backdrop of a blue sky, I couldn't help but wonder, "Is this real?" It was such a stunning sight that I felt like nature itself was woven from consciousness, almost like a dream. "Is this real?" I found myself asking again. Just then, a sudden gust of wind swept through, sending leaves swirling around me. Out of the corner of my eye, I spotted one leaf landing oddly, flattening out in an unusual way as it touched the ground. Among the fallen leaves, some were yellow, and as I approached to examine this particular one closely, I marveled at how perfectly it was shaped — it looked just like something one would draw.

Sunlight streamed through the trees, creating beautiful patterns as the branches danced in the warm wind. The leaf was golden with tawny brown edges and speckled with bits of gray dirt. It looked flawless. I quickly scanned the other fallen leaves; some were the same size and color, but none were quite like this one — it was so flat. I bent down to get a closer look, filled with a sense of wonder mixed with excitement and nervousness as I reached out for it. Suddenly, a strong gust of wind blew again, and while the other leaves were whisked away, this one remained still — until the wind surged again, lifting it and revealing what lay beneath it.

To my astonishment, I discovered a white fuzzy body with legs and antennae, struggling to maintain its balance. It was a stunning moth! As the wind calmed down, I could see her — a gold-colored moth that blended perfectly with the leaves surrounding her. I pulled out my iPhone and began recording this magnificent creature from different angles, reflecting on what had just happened. Then it suddenly struck me. What was I thinking about when the leaves started fluttering down around me? "Is this real?"

It was real, and beneath that leaf-like exterior was a complex creature — a moth that had evolved to mimic the leaves of this tree, right down to the gradients of yellow and bronze patina with specks of white and gray. The appearance of the golden moth felt like a response from the Universe, as if it were saying, "Yes, it's all real, but it's not what it seems." The appearance of the moth perfectly answered my earlier question, and I was in awe of the timing of it all. According to Jung, synchronicities are meaningful coincidences between an inner psychological event and an outer physical event. I had just experienced a classic Jungian synchronicity down to the golden insect. As this realization washed over me, the amazing "leaf" suddenly took flight and literally flew away.

The world is indeed real, yet it often masks a deeper truth. What I thought was a dead leaf was actually a golden Japanese silk moth. The illusion is real, but the truth is behind the appearances.

Breaking the Fourth Wall

When the sun shines down on Susanoo after finding the magical sword, it's a synchronous event. When one's life becomes in sync with something greater than one's self, it feels meaningful. Like the phases of the moon, or the planets aligning in astrology coinciding with one's personal growth. The narrative world and the objective world touch. The meta-story and one's own story. Where the pattern meets possibility. Poetry and life. *It is in between two worlds, where meaning is born.*

There's a fundamental symmetry between our inner experiences and the external world, suggesting that the patterns we see in our thoughts and feelings align with a larger, transcendent truth. Jung suggested that the collective unconscious communicates with us through dreams and by influencing events in the external world, a phenomenon he referred to as synchronicity. He believed that the coincidences, premonitions, and patterns we occasionally notice are actually messages from the unconscious — whether from our individual psyche or that of a larger group, such as our family, friends, community, culture, or even humanity as a whole, the planet, the cosmos. These experiences attract our conscious attention and aim to steer us, guide us, while revealing insights about the hidden depths surrounding us.

The collective unconscious operates through fundamental templates that reflect the natural ways the Mind of Nature expresses itself, akin to harmonics and resonant frequencies. Archetypes serve as the basic patterns of behavior, representing how the psyche naturally unfolds. We are all patterns of energy aligned with these behavioral templates. We may choose to overlook these archetypal patterns at our own peril, but they ultimately cannot be dismissed.

Archetypes can reveal themselves through images, emotions, and behavioral patterns, each symbolizing or conveying a deeper message. Like the harmonics of guitar strings, archetypes represent the vibrational essence of Universal Mind. These archetypes extend beyond the depths of the human mind and into the very essence of nature. The behaviors of everything in nature — animals and plants, mountains and rivers, suns and moons, fire and rain — seem to resonate with the archetypal patterns found in our own minds.

When an archetype is activated by certain circumstances, it manifests across both the observer's mind and the underlying consciousness of the physical world, resulting in significant coincidences. This alignment occurs because both our inner psyche and the outer world are expressions of Mind of Nature. If what exists within us is a fragment of Universal Mind, and the physical world outside is also part of that Universal Mind, it makes sense that there would be moments of coincidence between the two. Synchronicity is beyond our mind's natural tendency to create narratives. It embodies the harmony of these inner and outer resonances — a kind of dance of Mind with Itself. The archetypal tone adds a feeling of destiny to these experiences.

I have a beautiful *suibokuga,* a traditional Japanese ink wash painting that my friend's master student had painted at a live painting event, hanging on my wall for the past decade. It's a painting of a crane wading in a pond at night, looking up at the full moon. Ink wash paintings typically use just black ink, but the artist added a striking dash of red on the crane's crown. I love this painting and look at it every day; it has become a guiding principle.

At first glance, the moon appears to be an object within the painting, but when one looks closely, one realizes it's the only part that hasn't been painted — it's simply the white paper. I remember that the first thing the artist did was place a bucket on the *washi,* traditional Japanese paper, and then spray ink around it. When he lifted the bucket, a perfect white circle remained. The moon isn't really part of the landscape; it exists outside the space occupied by the other elements in the painting. So, while the moon seems like an object in the scene, it's actually a portal into the true reality of the landscape — the white paper itself. God is like the canvas; without it, there can be no painting. In this crane painting, the full moon serves as a gateway to the sacred.

Synchronicity resembles the moon in the painting; it reveals a fragment of truth — an epiphany, a miracle, a doorway to the transcendent. It's like getting a glimpse of God, but maybe it's just his back. If one were to see God's face, it would mean they're dead. Just as the crane directs its gaze at the full moon, this painting points to something greater. It illustrates the awareness breaking through. Synchronicity is a unique experience, alongside meditation and introspection, which grants us access to the true nature of the universe, allowing us to see beyond its mere surface.

One of the first lessons actors learn in film is to avoid looking directly into the camera, as that breaks the fourth wall — the imaginary barrier that separates the performers from the audience. In theater, this wall separates the actors from the audience, while in film and television, it's represented by the camera lens. Occasionally, breaking this wall can serve as a creative element, as we've seen in movies like *Deadpool* or *Annie Hall*. Similarly, a moment of synchronicity feels like breaking the fourth wall with God. In those instances, we, as the observer, suddenly receive a direct message from the divine. As an Indian sage once said, to see the world is to see God, and to see God beyond our world is to understand our own divine nature.

In the fall of 2023, I was getting ready to film a music video for my spoken word project *Dragon of Possibility: Act 1 Spoken Things* at a location called Kofuji, or "little Fuji," about halfway up Mount Fuji, which usually offers a stunning view of the sunrise. For a few months, I had been rehearsing with my director of photography at Saigoyama-koen, a park in Shibuya with a steep climb similar to Kofuji and I was eager to get started. I had been writing for years and this poem formed the foundation of this very book. After a month of memorizing and planning for the shoot, I found out just a week before that the road up the mountain was closing for winter, weeks earlier than expected and we lost our location. It was a setback, but I didn't want to lose momentum. My girlfriend suggested Aokigahara Forest, and during my research, I discovered a small shrine called the Dragon Cave, which was home to a dragon goddess deep within the forest. It seemed like the perfect place to shoot my video — what better setting than inside a dragon cave?

We traveled to Yamanashi, where we located the nearest access point into the forest. We drove as far as we could before parking and continuing on foot. When we finally reached the cave, it took my breath away. The rocks were covered in lush green moss, and the cave entrance had a stunning cliff-like overhang. It was clear that we had found the perfect location for my poetry film. A few weeks later, we gathered a dedicated crew of four to shoot inside the Sea of Trees at the Dragon Cave. Our plan was to film in four different areas around the dragon's lair. Before we started, we each took a moment to pay our respects to the dragon goddess at the shrine deep within the cave, and asked for her blessing. The location was enchanting, and the afternoon light was just perfect. We had just enough time before sunset to capture all the shots we needed.

We were about halfway through the shoot, making our way down a path alongside a field of *susuki*, tall Japanese silver grass, when suddenly, from the top of a hill to our left, a magnificent stag with huge antlers appeared. It was startling because he bolted toward us with such energy, then suddenly just halted dead in its tracks. We all froze, surprised, gazing at the majestic buck as it stared back at us with a glint in its eye. After about twenty seconds, the stag gracefully pranced down the hill, pausing once more to look back at us, its elegant antlers outlined against the golden susuki field, before dashing back into the dense woods from where it had come.

The crew exchanged awed glances, mesmerized by the encounter, feeling incredibly fortunate to have seen such a wild creature up close. In that moment, it felt as if the dragon goddess had taken on a new form to greet us, blessing the shoot and allowing us to have a meaningful experience. We resumed our work, blocking our next shot and continued to film. It was only later, on the drive home, that I truly appreciated the amazing symbolism of that awesome experience.

The stag is a powerful literary motif representing the sacred. In the classic Studio Ghibli film, *Princess Mononoke,* there's a pivotal moment for the young prince Ashitaka, when he encounters the *Shishigami,* the God of the Forest — a majestic deer god with many antlers. Similarly, in HBO's *House of the Dragon,* Princess Rhaenyra sees a white stag, symbolizing that she is the rightful heir to the Iron Throne. Deer often serve as symbols of a connection to the supernatural; they are messengers. When you're on the right path, you might spot a deer.

Afterwards, we made our way to another area of the forest to film in a susuki field. The silver shining susuki fields are a Japanese motif, being the backdrop of one of my favorite films, the 1964 Japanese historical drama, *Onibaba,* about two women who ambush and kill samurai to sell their armor. On a particularly tricky long take, my stylist Yoppy, who was also our spirit mascot and acted as a camera assistant, dove into a patch of tall, thick susuki reeds. After we yelled, "Cut!" he sprang up, brandishing a beautiful, complete antler in his hand and exclaimed, "Look what I found!" Finding antlers is often seen as a sign of upcoming prosperity, and Yoppy certainly deserved this moment. The deer is a powerful symbol found in mythologies and literature around the world. The stag, as a spirit animal, embodies the concept of being in an "in-between" state, connecting the worlds of dreams and wakefulness — the realm of intuition. Just as the fairy-like fawns blossom flowers from their antlers in Alex Garland's *Annihilation,* antlers are thought to guide us toward higher awareness, acting as spiritual antennae that encourage us to be more attuned to our inner thoughts and perceptions.

I'm holding Yoppy's antler in one of the final shots. The shoot turned out to be one of those perfect shoots — a real gift from the film gods — where not a single piece of footage was wasted. Everything we filmed fit perfectly; each location was exactly what we needed, and I'm extremely proud of the final piece. Encountering the stag felt like a meta-coincidence, considering that the deer is a literal motif symbolizing the "in-between," which is exactly the theme of the poem we were shooting. It was a moment of archetypal synchronicity. These symbolic reflections represent the "correspondences" between the natural and spiritual worlds. When one's personal potential intersects with the greater whole — the universal pattern, the Deer God, the Spirit of the Forest — it creates an ebb and flow of meaning, a reminder of the inextricable bond between mind and world.

Jung described synchronistic events as acts of creation. In our world, there exists a place where new things emerge, where creative acts and synchronistic events signify the meeting of heaven and earth. In between two worlds, here and the beyond. The inner unknown inside conversing with the outer unknown that lies beyond. Meeting my deer while shooting *Dragon of Possibility* was a moment of creation within a creation, and it was truly beautiful. It was a spectrum of experience.

Double Meaning

The dragon that consumes its own tail is known as the Ouroboros, an ancient symbol of renewal and transformation — representing both death and rebirth. On a psychological level, what helps one navigate an encounter with this dragon is one's ability to let go of what no longer serves oneself, allowing it to die and then be reborn. If one confronts one's fears, one'll come out okay. The part of one's self that's no longer necessary will die. This is similar to Tanjiro's experience in the hit manga and anime series *Kimetsu no Yaiba*'s movie, where he repeatedly dies and awakens in his dreams, each time facing death until he ultimately gains the strength to conquer his fears.

After experiencing the blue heart in the sky, I woke up the next morning — on my birthday — to a fantastic surprise: I was offered the role of the main antagonist, Lyon Arkland, who transforms into Kamen Rider Zaia in a "V-Cinema" movie. V-cinema films are a little bit edgier than the typical Kamen Rider movie. It was the perfect birthday gift. Even my friends and fellow Canadians, Monkey Majik, contributed to the film by lending their voices to the A.I. and providing music for the soundtrack. I feel incredibly honored to portray a character who transforms into a Kamen Rider, especially a Dark Rider — a childhood dream come true. There's something delicious about playing the bad guy; it allows one to explore a darker side of oneself. The filmmakers encouraged me to come up with my own choreography for my transformation into Kamen Rider mode. The theme for my character Kamen Rider Zaia was two dinosaurs: the Triceratops and the Carnotaurus. *Tokusatsu* (special effects) films, like *Godzilla* and *Kamen Rider*, are iconic in Japan and have a significant cultural impact around the world. I never could have imagined that I would be able to partake in such an exciting and fun experience. It was my first mainstream role in the Japanese entertainment industry in over ten years.

The greatest pattern is the story of transformation. We all go through it. Maybe you're going through it now. When one makes mistakes, those experiences make one wiser. It is the dawn of something new — the new version of oneself. That's the key: to let go of the past and be reborn. One transforms, like in *Dragon Ball, Pokémon,* or *Kamen Rider*. Just as the phoenix rises from the ashes, burning off what is no longer needed and allowing a better version of ourselves to emerge, filled with gratitude. This theme of death and rebirth runs deep in our myths and resonates throughout culture. We are all, whether we know it or not, playing a part in this universal narrative every day. We learn from our mistakes, striving to rebuild ourselves into something stronger. Sometimes, a little death is necessary for growth. True transformation happens only when the old form passes away, making way for something new.

We all love a Cinderella story in sports. Who can resist cheering for the underdog team that wasn't even meant to be at the dance? Renowned American author Kurt Vonnegut discusses the shapes of stories. The classic tale of *Cinderella,* also known as *The Little Glass Slipper,* follows a compelling pattern that captivates us every time. At the start, Cinderella is stuck in a terrible situation, living as a servant with her cruel stepmother and mean stepsisters. But then, her fortunes change with a magical pumpkin carriage and a beautiful dance with the prince. Just when it seems she's found happiness, the clock strikes midnight, leading to a dramatic fall where everything appears lost. Yet, it's only after this low point that she finally experiences her greatest happily-ever-after.

This pattern reflects a classic narrative structure: a descent followed by a re-ascent. It's like the Japanese pitch pronunciation, Ta•tsu•to. Shoutout to Dōgen. The pattern appears in countless narratives in the biblical corpus. In the Old Testament we see the story of Adam and Eve and their Fall from Paradise, Noah and the flood, Moses and the Exodus. Hope emerges in the New Testament with the star of Bethlehem and the birth of Jesus Christ, who comes to offer salvation. Then we face the unimaginable suffering of the Passion, and Good Friday, Christ's death. Yet, just as with *Cinderella,* there's a resurrection; the stone is rolled away, and on Easter Sunday, we celebrate the triumph of life over death. The deeper dive into suffering and pain is essential for experiencing the light.

The rising dragon spirals upward, serving as a perfect metaphor for life's journey. From the side, it appears linear and climbs vertically, but when viewed from above, a circular shape is revealed. Each time we return to the same point on this circle, it may feel like we are in the same place, but in reality, we are moving upward, closer to a higher state of being. With each return, there's an opportunity to see what we thought we understood during previous experiences, yet it's impossible to predict how we will feel when we arrive there again in the future — it's a new rung on the ladder. This duality of circularity and linearity allows us to witness both progress and return simultaneously. It's a gradual journey toward our goals, filled with mini deaths and resurrections that continue indefinitely, all spiraling upward toward something greater.

From the wound is a womb; we are all reborn through our vulnerabilities. Improvement requires sacrifice, we must become masters of letting go and embracing transformation. Take moments to reflect on where one started and understand that this journey is ongoing. We'll always find ourselves returning to familiar beginnings, but with a new perspective. The fountainhead of life isn't power or pleasure, or happiness; it's meaning. A meaningful event is one that enhances one's life and is purposeful, guiding one closer to one's goals. When one feels that something is meaningful, it means one is progressing and getting better. That sense of meaning can be a source of strength during tough times. Even just reflecting on one's experiences can be meaningful, as it fosters growth. At least one is looking in the mirror instead of blaming others.

Synchronicity is the intersection between the universal narrative pattern of transformation and the individual's potential for change. It is a meaningful moment of transformation that is created when the individual's potential aligns with the greater pattern of the universe. How to be better. To be a force of good in the world because the good in life is worth fighting for. We should notice and find coherence in these patterns. These coincidences can be valuable moments of change if we so choose. An instance of serendipitous grace can open up possibilities if one allows it to. It's a moment so profound, a reminder of one's ability to transform the world, for good or bad. That's why paying attention is important.

It was around 10 p.m. on a summer night and I was out on a run, Yoyogi Koēn was unusually empty. Earlier that day, I had finished writing the ending of this very book, and I was filled with a sense of elation and gratitude. As I ran, my mind began to wander to the nature of God, as it often does. What happened next was significant: I was asking a specific question in my mind. As I continued along the path, right beneath a lamp post, I stumbled upon an incredible sight — a stately guardian to the secret of my future. There, sitting under the light, was the silhouette of an unusually large cat, reminiscent of the Cheshire Cat from Lewis Carroll's *Alice in Wonderland*. At first, I wondered if it was a *tanuki*, a Japanese raccoon, a creature I had seen in the area before. But this figure was larger and fluffier, with pointy ears standing upright. It remained motionless as I cautiously approached, staring ahead in disbelief. As I drew nearer, the large cat turned its head slowly and fixed its bright yellow, unblinking eyes on me. To my astonishment, I realized it wasn't a cat at all, but a majestic nocturnal raptor — a Eurasian eagle-owl.

On that night, the great owl simply sat there, gazing back at me with those glowing yellow eyes and white feathers ruffling on its face. I stopped in my tracks, matching its gaze. In that moment, I felt as if I were peering into the essence of consciousness itself. I sensed that the owl was looking beyond the surface of my humanity, reaching deep into an unnamable foundation that I was just beginning to grasp. The act of being seen transformed me; my identity began to dissolve, leaving behind only the vibrant dialogue between us. I became the very essence of that exchange — the dance between what I perceived as "self" and what I considered "other." In that dissolution, both entities faded away, giving rise to an exhilarating ecstasy, a radiant presence emerging from that dissolving surface. Then, with a silent grace, the owl spread its enormous wings and lifted off the ground, disappearing into the night. My heart was pounding. I ran a little further away and crouched behind a bush, and after catching my breath, I made a hooting sound. To my surprise, the owl returned, and from my hide, I started taking video with my phone. As I filmed, I thought to myself, *what was I thinking and feeling just before the magical encounter occurred.*

Being sensitive to synchronicity is a way of life. Paying attention and listening is like living a secret story. Hunting for a feeling is a new way of taking in the world. When one is in sync with the pattern, it feels like one has a soundtrack to one's life. I did that literally recently and had a real-life *Dark Side of the Rainbow* experience. I pushed play on Coldplay's concept album *Moon Music* (2024) and went out and had an enlightening adventure that I'll never forget. Synchro in the city. When one pays attention, one is always in a meditative state. The heightened sensitivity to our surroundings, people, and what's going on around ourselves is our only salvation. However, it's important to avoid going overboard and finding meaning in everything, of course. Finding balance is key so one doesn't get overwhelmed by emotions or misled by false narratives. One should focus on cultivating trust in one's intuition as a guide.

All meaning is subjective and must be created by the individual. It's up to one to give one's life purpose and significance; one has to shine one's own light. Was it merely a random event, or is there a deeper story — a coincidence that holds meaning? By staying consistently aware, one can notice the subtle and quiet cues in life that point to countless possibilities right before one's eyes. Once an intention is set, an answer often comes out of the blue; the key is whether one can recognize it. As legendary music producer Rick Rubin states in *The Creative Act: A Way of Being,* one can't catch any fish if one hasn't cast a line. Always have one's line in the water.

It becomes clear that trusting in synchronicity is essential. That night, the owl was a messenger of my future, which was the writing I would do in that future. The encounter with my "bird of pray" was so deeply powerful that I was able to complete the book, a screenplay, and a novella. As I wrote, I felt that this was exactly what I should be doing — that Nature was expressing itself through me. These synchronicities felt like messages encouraging me to keep going, a sign that I was in harmony with the natural ebb and flow around me. Trust that what truly matters will come into one's life. By embracing this concept, one can navigate the waves of life with confidence. The universe responds when we harbor a genuine longing in our hearts and engage in thoughtful, reflective introspection.

The archetypal manifestations in our lives — both in dreams and waking moments — create a symbolic narrative that reveals what's happening in our unconscious mind. It's crucial to pay attention to these messages and to understand the meaning of the archetypes so that we can adjust our attitudes in our waking life. Our dreams, visions, passions, and spontaneous actions all hold significance that can be interpreted if we're attentive to them. What does the world around me signify? What do its images represent symbolically? What messages are they conveying? As Dr. Kastrup eloquently explains, idealism imbues our world and life itself with meaning. This meaning exists both figuratively, as in something happens for a purpose, like getting closer to a goal, and literally, in that what we see are just symbols, the world represents a deeper truth.

Like words — those marks of ink on paper — serving as symbols pointing towards something greater, our thoughts and perceptions too are encoded in ways and therefore they mean something, allowing us to find purpose in life. A meaningful life involves moving through the world with a curious mind, constantly asking oneself what things truly mean. What does nature represent? Being deeply engaged with these representations allows us to tap into our evolved capacity for self-reflection — our metacognition — gained over billions of years. This journey is about seeking understanding and drawing insights from our experiences. There is a profound richness of meaning all around us, just waiting to be discovered.

The moth, the stag, and the owl were representations of the corroboration between my inner and my outer experience. Like when we witness clouds drifting across the sky, or two birds swiftly flying by, it's reflecting a similar feeling within us. Often, we need to observe something in our surroundings to become aware of a change within ourselves. It's this conversation that creates meaning.

"To watch the sun, sink behind a flower clad hill. To wander on in a huge forest without thought of return. To stand upon the shore and gaze after a boat that disappears behind distant islands. To contemplate the flight of wild geese seen and lost among the clouds. And, subtle shadows of bamboo on bamboo." According to Zeami, all of these are portals to *yūgen*. Yūgen is described as "a profound, mysterious sense of the beauty of the universe ... and the poignant beauty of human suffering." Zeami associated yūgen with "refined elegance" in Noh performance. Literally meaning "dark" or "obscure," yūgen conveys a beauty that is only partially perceived, deeply felt yet barely glimpsed by the audience.

Zeami wrote, "The essence of yūgen is true beauty and gentleness." This beauty goes beyond mere appearances; it has to hint at something deeper behind the text and the noble gestures of the actors — a world that is impossible to define but undeniably real. These elements come together to embody the eternal passions of the soul, producing the ethereal quality known as yūgen. It represents a profound emotional awareness of the universe, suggesting something transcendent that isn't merely an allusion to another world. Instead, it invites us to engage with this world, to immerse ourselves in this experience, and to notice beauty.

Thread of Destiny

Doing the right thing at the right moment requires impeccable timing. The actor skillfully senses the audience's heightened excitement and anticipation, delivering his first line perfectly to capture their full attention. Zeami emphasizes the crucial role of mastering this timing. No matter how wise your words may be, if the timing is off, they won't truly resonate with others. We've all experienced failure because of poor timing — whether in negotiating a business deal or presenting a proposal to a superior. Zeami notes that timing involves understanding the shifts in the human mind. He further explains that we often miss the mark because we don't fully grasp the thoughts and feelings of others.

This timing connects us with nature and a deeper understanding of what God represents. If one possesses a "Flower" that opens up possibilities, one will be ready to seize opportunities when they arise. Intuition is hearing a possibility. To be able to apprehend the inside of what is being said to one's self. In our modern world, we've become so reliant on reason that we've lost touch with our intuitions. Yet, this instinctual connection represents the fundamental harmony of existence itself.

Nietzsche once said that every great person is the actor of their own ideal. To embody that ideal is the first step toward transforming into it. One's ideal is what one believes in, driving one's actions forward, while transformation is the result of those actions. One must actively live it out. If one embraces a certain role, one will evolve into the person one aspires to be. In this way, choice and action are one and the same.

The black-and-white double dragons of the yin-yang symbol are named Choice and Destiny. When our choices intersect with our destiny, we are in a good place. Our actions and words are part of our creative process; we have the power to steer our world closer to heaven or towards hell. This is where literal and metaphorical truths converge. We have the ability to shape reality for the better or worse — a rising dragon or a falling one; doing the right thing at the right moment is not easy.

The red thread of fate, often referred to as the "red string of destiny," is a captivating belief from Japanese folklore. It suggests that two people who are meant to be together are connected by an invisible red string tied to their pinky fingers. Although this string may twist or stretch, it can never break, representing the strong and enduring bond between these individuals. No matter the time, place, or circumstances, these two are destined to find each other and be together. This lovely and romantic concept has been celebrated in many forms of art, literature, and media. It also reflects an ancient notion that fate involves an invisible thread linking everything in the world and across time. Embracing the idea of fate can change our perspective on the world around us.

Archetypes are the universal laws of human fate. Each archetype is a living pattern with its own essence. Myths and gods continue to thrive in our collective unconscious. When one learns to understand these archetypal patterns, one can tap into their power. One can confront and grapple with the metaphorical dragon, channel its energy, corral it. One can ride the dragon and steer it in one's favor; life will bring both ups and downs, but one can learn to navigate those changes. We're like boats caught in a storm, navigating a sea of stories, while archetypes serve as the weather patterns. While we can't control the weather, we have our hands on the rudder and can make thoughtful decisions and take responsibility for the present moment we're in. Each individual is making a cosmic difference in the universe with every choice they make every day.

These patterns are woven into the very fabric of reality, universal archetypes that manifest in our individual minds and in the world around us. I believe that the narrative pattern is causal; it's not merely a story or a fiction – it's the essence of reality itself. It represents the possibility for reality to exist. Our ever-changing world is influenced by timeless, unchanging properties, and it's responding to those influences. Is the pattern divine? Suffering is the most profound aspect of life – there's nothing more real than pain. Yet it is this narrative pattern that enables us to transcend it. When we feel like we're falling apart, it's this very pattern that helps us come back together. We are like a living kimono, intricately woven brocade made from silk – the *Nishijin-ori,* to be precise. We resemble a living textile that requires a pattern or design, much like those finely woven fabrics. Without a design, we unravel and fall apart. Especially when we face challenges and feel truly lost, the threads of our being can unravel without a guiding design – the narrative structure of our lives. To be whole, we need meaning. When we connect with something larger than ourselves, we can overcome anything. And perhaps, if we're fortunate enough, we can become a high-quality kimono.

The crane wife's sacrifice was born out of love. When she plucked her own feathers and painstakingly wove a beautiful and delicate silk brocade, her actions were guided by love, aimed at ensuring another's happiness and well-being. "I love you. I want you to be happy," she conveyed, without any attachment. Making such sacrifices gives our lives meaning, and that meaning helps us cope with the inevitable suffering we all face. We might ask ourselves, "How can I be of service to others?" To make something sacred — that's the essence of what sacrifice really means. It involves suffering to create something sacred and meaningful. Through suffering, we gain insights and are confronted with universal truths that we might otherwise overlook. Suffering is an inherent part of Nature; it is as much a part of life as love.

I often visit a temple in Asagaya, where the *torii* entrance gates feature a rising dragon on the left column and a falling dragon on the right column. Don't get confused with where the dragons are positionally, it's the direction the head is pointing that determines its orientation. Whenever I feel lost, I find myself there, gazing up and praying to the Dragon God. I've wandered off track so many times. In my prayers, I try to ask good questions. What am I refusing to see that could guide me out of this difficult place? It's not easy to confront these truths, as they can be painful. Ryujin seems to be telling us, "You don't realize that I'm trying to help. I'm always doing my best to send you signs." Sometimes, I go to church and kneel before the crucifix to pray. The most powerful prayer one can offer isn't about asking for what one wants but rather seeking guidance on how to transform into a better vessel for divine will. God is always trying to communicate and find ways to help us become more aware.

Each person contributes a unique thread to the tapestry of history, woven together as we live and dream. When we immerse ourselves fully into the story trying to live through us, we have the opportunity to create something new. We can let ourselves resonate with the rhythm of Nature. When tuned in, the things worth thinking and writing about are right there. When one is present and engaged with the world around one's self, every now and then, inspiration strikes. It doesn't have to be a grand revelation; just be open and pay attention. What invisible help am I walking past right now? What am I missing?

Life is naturally poetic; it unfolds a story rich with meaning, expressed through vivid images. It is an open book meant to be read and interpreted, inviting us to connect deeply and evoke genuine emotions. By engaging with the images and narratives of our psyche, we can connect with our true selves, leading to a more profound and fulfilling experience of life. *We are all actor.*

The word *kokoro* in Japanese can be translated to mean both "mind" and "heart." Kokoro encompasses not just the cognitive functions of the mind but also the emotional and spiritual dimensions associated with the heart. Unlike in many Western contexts, where the mind and heart are often seen as distinct and sometimes even opposing forces, in Japanese thought, they are more integrated. The duality reflects the interconnectedness of thoughts and feelings in the human experience.

Emotions are an integral part of ethical reasoning. Emotional intelligence reveals its strong guiding potential, which can sometimes feel like it has a mind of its own. Few experiences besides reflecting on our emotions allow us to connect with the deeply human and recognize the presence of an inner life that functions independently of our conscious, rational mind. Emotions serve as the raw material for the co-creative process, the conversation between inner and outer, that counters the chaos we face.

When one considers how emotions arise as a part of human nature, at the same time as being a part of Mind of Nature itself, it makes one wonder if these emotions truly belong to us or represent the suffering of the world, guiding us to feel and respond on its behalf. In this sense, our feelings may be the world's way of communicating with us, making them an essential aspect to "co-creation" — a synergy between self-awareness, transformation, and a cosmology of consciousness. Recognizing the independent intelligence of these deep emotional responses could be an invitation to align ourselves with Mind of Nature.

God needs us. We are the wise ape holding up a mirror to God, reflecting divine actions. The meaning of life is understanding that God is nature — instinctive and spontaneous. However, through our ability to reflect, to think and feel, make moral judgments, and discern justice from injustice — good from evil — this allows nature to confront the outcomes of its own reflexive behavior. This is why we're alive, this interaction is the essence of life's meaning.

The word for ephemeral in Japanese is *hakanai,* which evokes moments in threat of a quick death like the transitory existence of a cherry blossom or the life of a samurai heading into battle. The kanji for hakanai is a combination of the characters for "dream" and "man," symbolizing the dream of God — inviting us to experience one moment of beauty through our own eyes, no matter how brief it may be.

I blew out the five colorful candles on my birthday cake and heard the roar of all my friends and family, cheering me on. I turned around and hugged my mother tightly. Later that night, we watched *Folktales in Japan* together. *Tatsu no ko Tarō* rides a majestic dragon on the screen, and for a moment, I feel like I am Taro the Dragon Boy. Mother of Dragon now resides in Victoria, British Columbia, just a two-minute stroll from the beach. In front of her kitchen sink, there's an oval-shaped window that offers a lovely view of the garden, complete with a hummingbird feeder that attracts many sweet-beaked visitors. She says, occasionally, a Steller's blue jay will stop by, just as she was wondering how I'm doing. She'll even talk to the blue bird and say a little prayer for me. I'll leave you with some wise words from Maman:

"Today, tonight, rising dragon or falling dragon?"

It's up to U.

Epilogue

Seahorses are known for their lifelong pair bonding. Each morning, the male and female come together to go for a promenade with tails entwined. They engage in a ritual dance, swirling around each other in a display of graceful synchrony. As they move, they change colors, allowing them to gauge each other's reproductive readiness.

Seahorses are among the only animals on Earth where the male goes through pregnancy and labor. Shortly after the male gives birth to tiny, fully independent offspring, the female is already prepared with new eggs, and they quickly mate again.

Male pregnancy means the male is certain he's the father, which may be why male seahorses are so involved.

Author Biography

JAI TATSUTO WEST is a half Japanese, half French-Canadian actor, screenwriter, and poet, born in Vancouver, BC, and based in Tokyo for over 25 years. He has appeared in numerous films and television shows in North America and Japan, making his screen debut in 1991 on the popular show *21 Jump Street*. In 2004, he co-starred in the Japanese box office hits *Survive Style 5+*, *The Private Detective Mike*, and *Hazard*. In 2018, he became the Chairman of *Iron Chef Canada*. He has also released two spoken word poetry albums in English and Japanese under the pseudonym *Lotus Chamelion*. West is the lead actor in a new Sion Sono film entitled *Evaporation*.

Bibliography

Barfield, Owen. *Saving the Appearances: A Study in Idolatry*. United Kingdom: Faber & Faber, 1957.

Benedict, Ruth. *The Chrysanthemum and the Sword: Patterns of Japanese Culture*. Cleveland: Meridian Books, 1967.

Bettelheim, Bruno. *The Uses of Enchantment: The Meaning and Importance of Fairy Tales*. New York: Knopf, 1976.

Bishop, Paul. *Analytical Psychology and German Classical Aesthetics: Goethe, Schiller, and Jung*. East Sussex: Routledge, 2008.

Cameron, Julia. *The Artist's Way: A Spiritual Path to Higher Creativity*. New York: Penguin Group, 1992.

Campbell, Joseph. *The Power of Myth*. New York: Anchor Books, 1988.

Clarke, J.J. *Jung and Eastern Thought: A Dialogue with the Orient*. London: Routledge, 1994.

Davidson, Alan. *The Oxford Companion to Food*. London: Oxford University Press, 1999.

Doty, James R. *Into the Magic Shop: A Neurosurgeon's Quest to Discover the Mysteries of the Brain and the Secrets of the Heart*. New York: Avery, 2016.

Fry, Stephen. Interview on CBC News: *The National*. 2018.

Goleman, Daniel, and Richard Davidson. *The Science of Meditation: How to Change Your Brain, Mind and Body*. New York: Penguin Books, 2017.

Harpur, Patrick. *The Philosophers' Secret Fire: A History of the Imagination*. London: Arkana, 1994.

Hesse, Hermann. *Siddhartha: An Indian Novel*. New York: New Directions Publishing, 1951.

Hillman, James. *The Soul's Code: In Search of Character and Calling*. New York: Random House, 1996.

Hollis, James. *A Life of Meaning: Relocating Your Center of Spiritual Gravity*. Boulder: Sounds True, 2023.

Isbell, Lynne. *The Fruit, the Tree, and the Serpent: Why We See So Well*. New York: University of Chicago Press, 2020.

Jacobi, Jolande. *The Psychology of C.G. Jung*. Princeton: Princeton University Press, 1973.

Jones, David E. *An Instinct for Dragons*. New York: Routledge, 2002.

Jung, C.G. *Answer to Job*. Princeton: Princeton University Press, 1952.

Jung, C.G. *The Archetypes and the Collective Unconscious*. Princeton: Princeton University Press, 1959.

Jung, C.G. *Man and His Symbols*. New York: Doubleday, 1964.

Jung, C.G. *Synchronicity: An Acausal Connecting Principle*. Princeton: Princeton University Press, 1973.

Kastrup, Bernardo. *Decoding Jung's Metaphysics: The archetypal semantics of an experiential universe*. Winchester: Iff Books, 2016.

Kastrup, Bernardo. *More Than Allegory: On religious myth, truth and belief*. Winchester: Iff Books, 2016.

Kastrup, Bernardo. Interview with *Adventures in Awareness* (podcast), "With Reality in Mind."

Kawai, Hayao. *Dreams, Myths & Fairy Tales in Japan*. New York: Penguin Books, 1991.

Kawai, Hayao. *The Interface of Science and Religion*. Tokyo: Iwanami Shoten, 1986. (In Japanese.)

Kawai, Hayao. *The Japanese Psyche: Major Motifs in the Fairy Tales of Japan*. New York: Harper & Row, 1984.

Kingsnorth, Paul. *The Vaccine Moment: Covid, Control and the Machine*. 2022. www.paulkingsnorth.net.

Koestler, Arthur. *The Roots of Coincidence*. New York: Random House, 1972.

Lewis, C.S. *Miracles: A Preliminary Study*. New York: Macmillan, 1947.

Meade, Michael. *Fate and Destiny: The Two Agreements of the Soul*. MA: GreenFire Press, 2010.

McGilchrist, Iain. *The Matter with Things*. London: Perspectiva Press, 2021.

Miyao, Daisuke. *Sessue Hayakawa: Silent Cinema and Transnational Stardom*. Duke University Press, 2007.

Neumann, Erich. *The Origins and History of Consciousness*. Princeton: Princeton University Press, 1954.

Nihon Bungaku Kenkyū Shiryō Kankōkai. *Kojiki. Nihon Shoki*. Tokyo: Yuseido Shuppan.

Noguchi, Yoné. *The American Diary of a Japanese Girl*. New York: Frederick A. Stokes, 1901.

O'Gieblyn, Meghan. *God, Human, Animal, Machine*. New York: Doubleday, 2021.

Oida, Yoshi. *The Invisible Actor*. London: Routledge, 1994.

Okakura, Kakuzo. *The Awakening of Japan*. New York: The Century Co., 1904.

Peterson, Jordan. *Beyond Order: 12 More Rules for Life*. Toronto: Random House Canada, 2021.

Peterson, Jordan. *Maps of Meaning: The Architecture of Belief*. Toronto: Random House Canada, 1999.

Peterson, Jordan. "Maps of Meaning" Lecture Series [YouTube]. 2017.

Peterson, Jordan. "The Psychological Significance of the Biblical Stories" Lecture Series [YouTube]. 2017.

Rilke, Rainer Maria. *Letters to a Young Poet*. Translated by Mark Harman. Cambridge: Harvard University Press, 2011.

Rubin, Rick. *The Creative Act: A Way of Being*. New York: Penguin Press, 2023.

Sacks, Oliver. *The Man Who Mistook His Wife for a Hat and Other Clinical Tales*. London: Gerald Duckworth, 1985.

Sanford, John A. *The Invisible Partners*. New York: Harper & Row, 1980.

Shibusawa, Tatsuhiko. *Happiness is Forever Only for Women*. Tokyo: Kawade Shobō, 2006. (In Japanese.)

Slater, Glen. *Jung vs Borg: Finding the Deeply Human in a Posthuman Age*. Arroyo Grande: Winter Press, 2024.

Spira, Rupert. *Adventures in Awareness* (podcast interview, with Bernardo Kastrup). 2021.

Stanislavski, Konstantin. *An Actor Prepares*. New York: Theatre Arts Books, 1936.

Stanislavski, Konstantin. *Building a Character*. New York: Theatre Arts Books, 1949.

Stanislavski, Konstantin. *Creating a Role*. New York: Theatre Arts Books, 1961.

Storr, Anthony. *The Essential Jung*. London: Fontana Press, 1998.

Tolle, Eckhart. *The Power of Now: A Guide to Spiritual Enlightenment*. Novato, CA: New World Library, 1999.

Tsuji, Shizuo. *Japanese Cooking: A Simple Art*. Tokyo: Kodansha Intl., 1980.

Tufte, Virginia. *Artful Sentences: Syntax as Style*. Cheshire, CT: Yale University Press, 2006.

Von Franz, Marie-Louise. *On Divination and Synchronicity: The Psychology of Meaningful Chance*. Toronto: Inner City Books, 1980.

Waldron, William S. *Making Sense of Mind Only: Why Yogacara Buddhism Matters*. Somerville, MA: Wisdom Publications, 2023.

West, Jai T. *By Dusk*. 2017. Unproduced screenplay.

West, Jai T., and Dean Whiteside. *Choco Bon Bon: The Rise and Fall of a Japanese Pimp*. 2008. Unproduced screenplay.

Westwell, Chantry. *Dragons, Heroes, Myths & Magic*. London: The British Library, 2021.

Whyte, David. *David Whyte: Still Possible*. Langley, Washington: Many Rivers Press, 2022.

Zeami. *The Flowering Spirit: Classic Teachings on the Art of Nō*. Translated by William Scott Wilson. Boston: Shambhala, 1986.

Zeami. *Fūshikaden*. Tokyo: Iwanami Shoten, 1958. (In Japanese.)

***evo*Lve**

www.jaiwest.com

ESSENTIA

Essentia Books, a collaboration between Collective Ink Ltd. and Essentia Foundation, publishes rigorous scholarly work relevant to metaphysical idealism, the notion that reality is essentially mental in nature. For more information on modern idealism, please visit www.essentiafoundation.org.

Recent Bestsellers from Essentia Books Are:

Irreducible
Federico Faggin
The inventor of the microprocessor explores
the fundamental nature of consciousness.
Paperback: 978-1-80341-509-3 ebook: 978-1-80341-510-9

The Sapient Cosmos
James B. Glattfelder
Novel paradigms in physics and philosophy are
uncovering radical new visions for the ultimate
nature of reality and consciousness.
Paperback: 978-1-80341-404-1 ebook: 978-1-80341-405-8

Children's Unexplained Experiences in a Post Materialist World
Donna Maria Thomas
Paperback: 978-1-80341-084-5 ebook: 978-1-80341-085-2

Mind, Matter and Life
Massimiliano Sorrentino and Daniela Panighetti
Why the mind-matter problem could invalidate the neo-Darwinian materialist conception of the world.
Paperback: 978-1-80341-530-7 ebook: 978-1-80341-613-7

What Lies Beyond
Matt Colborn
Paranormal experiences — why they matter and
how they can help make a better tomorrow.
Paperback: 978-1-80341-829-2 ebook: 978-1-80341-836-0

In Pursuit of the Inconceivable

Peter Guy Jones

A comprehensive explanation of the relationship between formal scholastic metaphysics and the philosophical foundation of mysticism and the Perennial philosophy.

Paperback: 978-1-80341-906-0 ebook: 978-1-80341-921-3

Find more titles at

www.collectiveinkbooks.com/essentia-books

TRABAJEMOS *en familia*

50 IDEAS PARA ACTIVAR
A LOS TUYOS Y HACER
UNA DIFERENCIA

RICH BROWN Y ELISA SHANNON

e625.com

e625.com
TRABAJEMOS EN FAMILIA
Rich Brown y Elisa Shannon

Publicada por especialidades625® © 2019
Dallas, Texas Estados Unidos de América.

ISBN 978-1-946707-19-2

Todas las citas Bíblicas son de la Nueva Biblia al Día (NBD).

Editado por: Virginia Bonino de Altare
Diseño de portada e interior: Creatorstudio.net

Contenido